Gar-Field Hig
14000 Smoketown Road
Woodbridge, VA 22192

MW01118444

PETE NEWELL'S
DEFENSIVE BASKETBALL:
WINNING TECHNIQUES
AND STRATEGIES

PETE NEWELL

**Foreword by
Tara VanDerveer**

COACHES
CHOICE™

The Art & Science of Coaching Series

T 48126

©2001 Coaches Choice Books. All rights reserved. Printed in the United States.

No part of this book may be reproduced, stored in a retrieval system, or transmitted, in any form or by any means, electronic, mechanical, photocopying, recording, or otherwise, without the prior permission of Coaches Choice.

ISBN: 1-58518-332-6
Library of Congress Number: 00-108304

Book layout and cover design: Paul W. Lewis
Front cover photo: University of California, Berkeley, Sports Information Office
Inside photo of Pete Newell: Steve Hathaway
Research Editor: Mike Dunlap

Coaches Choice
P.O. Box 1828
Monterey, CA 93942
www.coacheschoiceweb.com

DEDICATION

This book is dedicated to Florence Newell
and all coaches' spouses
and players' mothers everywhere.

ACKNOWLEDGMENTS

My thanks go out to Lorraine Bispo, my typist, and Mike Dunlap, who provided invaluable research. Without all your efforts, this book would never have been possible.

                                                              ___P.N.

CONTENTS

For years, I have been a student and friend of Pete Newell. More than a few times, we have X and O-ed our way through a Chinese dinner, through the fortune cookies and tea, and well past the time when most alert people would have noticed that the management was giving clear signals that our patronage was no longer welcome. From these sessions and from my attendance at Pete's Big Man Camp and numerous clinics, I have come to respect Pete as an enigma of coaching. He possesses the talents of master teacher, parsimonious communicator and unconventional motivator.

In order to be a great teacher, one must possess a clear vision of *what* they want their players to do, *why* the players should execute in the manner proscribed, and *how* to teach the players to acquire these skills in the most efficient manner. Pete has an uncanny understanding of the technology of basketball. He knows exactly what he wants to see, and he knows what will happen when the skill is executed correctly—and what will happen if it is either omitted or performed incorrectly. More rare than his vision of basketball execution is his use of teaching strategies and communication genius which enable players to see the picture, understand the rules and master the skills in a minimum amount of instructional time.

As well as his teaching prowess, Pete is an icon of the game because he gives back to basketball so generously. He is respected by his peers and venerated by his players. His approach is an unusually positive one. Make no mistake, Pete is as demanding of players as the most tyrannous of his colleagues, but only in that he does not quit teaching until his players execute in the manner to which he ahs envisioned. Rather than punishing his players for mistakes, he teaches and re-teaches until there is success. The motivation, of course, is that his players so respect this man that they give their best effort in order to please their teacher.

Pete Newell is a legend of the game. His teams at the University of Sand Francisco were always in the mix at the end of the season. More recently, he has become the guru of post players. It is, perhaps, less well known that Pete's teams stayed at the top of the rankings every season because of their defensive play. Through innovation and flare, the University of San Francisco ushered into the game of basketball a new philosophy of pressure defense. His championships, which include the Big Three—NCAA Championship, NIT Championship, and Olympic Gold Medal—were all predicated on aggressive defense. It is fitting then that this book returns to Pete's roots.

Because Pete's text presents his way, readers of this book will find that no stone is left unturned in exploring the genesis of great defenses, the methods of teaching defensive skills to athletes, and the relationship between defense and its more glamorous counterpart. *Pete Newell's Defensive Basketball: Winning Techniques and Strategies* is certain to become "the bible" of defensive-minded students/teachers of the game.

Tara VanDerveer
Head Women's Basketball Coach
Stanford University

It is with pride that I associate myself with a game that was born in the United States and is today considered to be the fastest-growing team sport in the entire world. Basketball's growth in Europe has steadily increased since it was first introduced as an Olympic sport in Berlin at the 1936 Olympics. The popularity in Asia is beyond anyone's expectation, particularly in China, where it is considered to be the most popular sport in that country. Likewise in the Philippines and Korea, where basketball is a very popular television favorite and is the main team sport in those countries. The quality of play and enthusiasm for basketball in Australia is another example of its growing international popularity. American coaches have helped develop a game in which all nations can be competitive and can enjoy as spectators.

Basketball was, and is, a game of change. It's a game of counters that is constantly guided by rules and interpretations of these rules. It's a game of many balances; the penalty of the foul and the value of the ball possession is an example. Basketball's history shows us that there have been periods of imbalance, but we have been able to create change through new rules and interpretations. A study of its history shows the college coach, by experimentation of new rules proposals, has always steered the course of the game's direction.

Basketball as a series of games within a game is in evidence when examining the major rules changes that have impacted the way the game is played. Its great growth began with the institution of what is now the National Association of Basketball Coaches (NABC). We owe so much to our early leaders: Phog Allen of Kansas, Nat Holman of City College of New York, Henry Iba of Oklahoma A & M, Doc Carlson of Pittsburgh, Sam Barry of the University of California and Nibs Price of Cal-Berkeley. These were the leaders who gave our game the early direction by instituting the NABC and, in the case of Sam Barry and Nibs Price, volunteering their conference, the Pacific Coast Conference, to allow the experimentation of the elimination of the center jump after each made basket and, later, the installation of the 10-second midcourt line. These two rules forever changed the play of the game, both offensively and defensively. Adapting to the new and quicker pace of the game was made necessary by these two new rules. Likewise, the shot clock created a change of tactics and strategy. Most recently, the adoption of the three-point shot had the greatest impact since the elimination of the jump ball in 1937. Many less meaningful — but nevertheless important to the growth of the game — rules give evidence that basketball is a game that will never be static and resistant to change when change is needed.

A parallel can be drawn between the amateur game and the NBA. The college and high school games have made many rules changes and interpretations these past decades, and the game was never more popular than it is today. On the other hand, the NBA has not made a significant change since the inauguration of the shot clock. The three-point shot was instituted by the former NBA-rival league, the ABA. The NBA game has serious problems, as the past five years have shown; it has become an inactive game. A game that was high-scoring, action-packed and exciting has deteriorated into a slow-moving game with little fast action compared to what it offered in the 1980s and before. It is no coincidence that this game has regressed and that at the same time no significant rule changes have been introduced. Basketball is a game of change and delicate balance that needs constant monitoring by the people involved in the technical aspects. The coaches today have been handed a wonderful game that is like a beautiful garden. As the garden needs constant care and attention to keep from becoming overrun with weeds, basketball needs the same care and attention to keep it on course.

___ Pete Newell

CHAPTER 1

INTRODUCTION

Since the inception of the game of basketball, the paths of offense and defense have differed over these many years. Initially, the creativity in the offensive phases far exceeded the growth and creativity in the defensive phases. In the first half-century or more of the game, defenses were considered standard in their operations.

The individual defense, termed "man-to-man," was the one most practiced and played. The switch defense slowly grew in popularity in the '30s and early '40s. During the same period, more coaches also invoked the zone defense. Clair Bee, the renowned creator of the 1-3-1 zone defense, brought prominence nationally to that zone-type defense. His Long Island University teams were annually among the top teams nationally. Penn State had many adherents to its 2-3 zone and was a very difficult opponent to play because of the execution of its zone defense. The switch defense was the featured defense of Stanford University when it won the NCAA championship in 1941. The success of these teams with the different defenses influenced the thinking of many less successful coaches and induced them to embrace a change in defensive concept. Mainly, however, the individual man-to-man defense was the most common defense of the majority of coaches prior to 1940.

The influence of new rules and changes in interpretation has forever affected the game of basketball offensively and defensively. When a new offensive rule is invoked, it will invariably have implications—sometimes deep implications—in the defensive aspects of play. We have seen numerous incidents of this happening in the past half century of basketball.

There is little doubt in my mind that the two rule changes instituted in the late '30s to help the offense caused more major changes to the defense. The first rule change was the "elimination of the center jump after each made basket" rule and allowed the team scored upon to be allowed immediately to put the ball in play at the baseline. This rule created a tempo of play that basketball had never previously enjoyed and gave the game a fluid, quick pace that appealed to the players and coaches but, even more, gave it spectator appeal. The fast break was born.

Soon after, the 10-second-line rule was imposed, which further increased the game's tempo. Prior to this change, teams would sometimes hold the ball in the backcourt rather than try to attack a defense, often a zone defense. With the installation of this 10-second rule at the midline, offenses had to hurry the ball up the backcourt. A time-clock rule was not conceived of at that time.

I mentioned the implications of these rules to the defense. The full-court defense first made its presence known in the middle and late '40s. Normally a major rule change does not immediately have a serious impact on the game. Coaches are generally leery about adjusting concepts until they better understand the full scope of the impact of their adjustments. World War II put basketball on hold because of the overriding concerns of the war effort and the national draft of the late '30s. Until the conclusion of the war in 1945, few changes occurred in the play of the game. The great majority of basketball coaches were in some branch of the services. Prior to and for several years after the war, changes in play and adjustments to the changes of the late 1930s were slow. As will be pointed out in this book, the inversion concept of position gave great impetus to the development of the press defense and its many variations. Today, the press defense is an integral part of many successful and championship teams. As has been previously mentioned, these defensive additions to the game were the result of a rule that was intended to help the offensive phase of basketball. New rules, however, must be fully examined, regardless of whether their obvious intent is to help the defense or the offense.

Another rule change that greatly affected high school and college basketball was a redefinition of the legal screen rule. Prior to the change, a legal screen had to abide by the "three-foot rule." The change allowed a screen to be set within inches of a defender. The "three-foot rule" was the position a screener must observe when setting a screen on a defender. Should contact occur within the three-foot area, the offensive screener was at fault and charged with an offensive foul. The purpose of the rule was to allow the defender room to go over or under the legal three-foot screen. In the East, the rule was observed and called more frequently than elsewhere in the country. Many teams visiting in the East from other areas of the country had to change their offenses because of the sensitivity to the three-foot rule by eastern officials. It should be noted that basketball at that time was far from universal in its interpretation of numerous rules. An example was the traveling rule. In the West, traveling was closely called, but in the East, it was loosely called. It wouldn't be until the late '60s and early '70s that basketball achieved any real national standardization of rules interpretation.

This change of the legal screen rule was responsible for the most popular single offense in the history of basketball—the motion offense. This offense was a refinement of Coach Henry Iba's passing game-type offense and was conceived by Coach Bobby Knight of Indiana. Coach Iba's motion offense involved more movement and less screening since the three-foot rule was enforced at that time. When the screen rule change occurred, Coach Knight refined the passing game to a motion offense that featured legal, solid, physical screens and a spacing of its players completely different offensively from what most teams employed at that time. In theory, the spacing of the offense was in the vicinity of the paint area and on each side of the paint. The shot was, and is, created coming from the basket area to the perimeter by the eventual shooter. A screen, usually a down screen, has freed the receiver for the pass reception and shot. The offense had great continuity and made full use of the new screen rule interpretation.

Later in the 1970s, the flex offense made its impact in college and high school basketball. Initially conceived by Carroll Williams, the Santa Clara coach, the flex offense was somewhat similar to the popular motion offense with a derivation or refinement of reverse action, which was popular in the '50s and '60s.

Accompanying these two offensive concepts of play was a concept not as widely accepted as motion or flex, but a formation of play similar to the those offenses. This third concept was termed the "T" formation or triangle. Its similarity to the other offenses was that its creation of the shot was dependent upon off-the-ball screens. The spacing resembled a triangle with one player at the foul line, two offensive teammates at the opposite sides of the low post with the pass entry from the wing position, and the fifth player above the foul-line circle in the middle of the court. Down and side screens by the triangle people created the open shot. This type of offensive formation had been used by coaches in various ways prior to the advent of the motion or flex sets and even before the screen rule change, but it became more popular and refined when the screen rule change occurred.

The effect of the screen rule change made the individual assigned defenses more difficult to effectively play. Changes in personnel began to occur as guards were called upon to screen bigger backline opponents. The size difference reduced guards' effectiveness, so stronger and bigger guards began to appear in the game. Types of screens—down screens, side screens and back screens—compounded problems for the individual defenders. The role of the offensive center radically changed in its primary responsibilities. The post-up center, with his teammates spaced from sideline to sideline and at the outside perimeter, was free to express his individual moves and game. Passing and feeding open teammates bounce passes to backdoor cutters or to the slashing cuts of the perimeter teammates were skills all centers were called upon to improve. Additionally, the ability to read open teammates at the perimeter or at the weakside wing area was a "must" for the competent post player—to recognize and hit with a quick, strong pass to the weakside. The role of the center now became that of a screener, and the bigger and, often, stronger body made for an effective screen. The other offensive contributions were to "pop out" after the effective screen for a quick turnaround shot in the paint or slightly below the foul-line area. Because the center player was in the paint area, offensive rebounding was extremely important.

The physical demands on and abilities of the center player changed the recruiting demands of the college coach. The immense popularity of these new offenses—motion and flex—has slowly but surely eroded the all-around ability to pass, develop an offensive post game and to create a face-up game 15 feet or more from the basket of the center player in today's high school and college programs. Additionally, many coaches at these levels of play know only the motion and flex offenses. The age-old axiom of "coach what you know and know what you coach" has caused many coaches to reject the earlier post center play that I have described. It is more than a coincidence that nearly half of today's NBA centers were not born in the USA.

Many of us thought the 3-point shot rule would cause a return of the post-up center play; the spacing would encourage the perimeter spacing, especially weakside. The re-adoption of post offenses has become popular but not to any large degree. Many 6' 10" to 7' 0" centers at the college level have had little or no schooling in the skills a post player must develop if a professional career is to be possible. Again, it is not the responsibility of a college coach to change his or her beliefs nor to prepare an individual for a pro career, but to do what best serves the coach in establishing a successful, winning program. The problem of learning to defend a post-up center is equally great. Defending a post-up player who possesses varied individual post moves, is adept at developing a shot—either set shot or a drive to the basket—requires individual defensive footwork, and other offensive elements of post play create needed adjustments and present problems to a defensive post player who has little experience in one-on-one defensive situations.

This contrary situation is but another example of how rules dictate the play of the game. The 24-second time clock and the "no-zone" rule condition the play of the NBA game, and the high school and college rules committees invoke rules that best serve their competition. It is interesting to note that amateur basketball has increased in national interest at all levels of play as their rules groups have inserted new rules and clarification or redefinition of existing rules to keep abreast of the game's changes. There is more national interest in the NCAA Final Four than in any other competition we have in any championships in the country. The NBA, on the other hand, has done very little to adjust its game to the needs the change in play often demands and has made few or no rule changes to keep their game the exciting, popular game of a decade ago. The drop in scoring and the disappearance of the fast-moving, up-tempo game characteristic of the NBA are the results of little attention paid to what the game of basketball—amateur and professional—has historically needed.

We have, in part, briefly explained the history of the various defenses and the evolution of the game. In the various changes of play, usually brought on by new rules and interpretations, we have tried to trace the reasons why defenses were broadened in their scope as basketball evolved in its play and grew in its importance in the national sports scene. Coaching has become more efficient and professional, and the basketball coach has been responsible for guiding the profession to the eminence it now enjoys.

There is probably less individual teaching of the defensive basics of basketball than we have ever seen. Offenses depend less on part-method teaching today; consequently, part-method defensive teaching has diminished. Team defenses depend more on change of defense from an assigned individual to a particular type zone or a variety of zones—from a normal, individual-assigned defense to a change of defensive tempo that quickly becomes more aggressive, more denying of entries and requiring an offensive adjustment immediately to respond to this change of pace. Press defenses are more apt to give one look and quickly change to another type, almost imperceptible in its change. To better meet these changes usually demands an offensive-team adjustment as it reads the change. These are some of the reasons for the increased emphasis as team change has become more popular and individual teaching less emphasized by the coaches.

If one constant exists in basketball, it is that the basic fundamentals don't change. What were the basics of fundamental footwork fifty or more years ago are the fundamentals of today. Foot skills of offensive individual play are little different from the past skills taught, and the demands of foot movement initially in defending the ball handler have not changed in these many years.

In teaching basketball, the importance of describing the "why" has never changed. The "why" is a fundamental in classroom teaching, and it is certainly important in teaching the basics of defensive play of basketball. While it is important to explain the "how" of performing a particular aspect of play, it is even more important for the basketball coach to explain the "why." It has been my experience that the player who understands the "why" will consistently respond correctly to the situation. Consistent response will usually result in a consistent defense.

In teaching individual defense, the "we and us" concept should be firmly ingrained in the player's mind. It is more than a coincidence that all forms of the media describe the happenings in a game as one individual's or several individuals' scoring "x" numbers of points and rebounds, but defensive plaudits are described as a team effort. While individuals are seldom singled out as leading the defensive efforts, credit is often given to a team's effective press defense, tight aggressive individual-assigned defense, a match-up zone, etc.

Offense can be played one-on-one, two-on-two and three-on-three. Seldom do we find more than three people involved in an offensive creation of a shot—a screener, a cutter and a passer. Contrarily, we cannot play defense effectively with fewer than five players. One lazy, individual-thinking defender can break down an entire defense by allowing his or her immediate opponent to penetrate the defense with a token, hand-reaching defensive effort. Simply stated, offense is the "I" or "me" of basketball, while defense is the "we" and "us" of the game—one player defending the ball and four teammates helping by proper vision, loud communication and being in helping positions.

The basketball coach should be conscious of explaining the "why" and making the individual players realize how interdependent they must be as a defensive team and the importance of the "we" and "us."

CHAPTER 2

DEFENSE: ITS EARLY GROWTH

More creativity and resourcefulness have occurred in *defense* since the inception of basketball than in any other part of the game. In the game's early stages of development, the assigned-individual defense was most commonly employed. Some zones appeared, but they were, for the most part, static, little-movement type defenses with few principles of play. As basketball became more popular as a participation sport with some spectator appeal, the assigned-individual defense was the most widely accepted and successful. In the mid-1930s, Clair Bee, the very successful coach at Long Island University which was then one of the national collegiate powers, introduced a new zone alignment—the 1-3-1. It was considered a revolutionary concept and opened the minds of other coaches for the creation of other zone concepts. Penn State was famous for its aggressive, tight 2-3 alignment and was considered one of the top defensive college teams of that era. It was a period of much half-court defense creativity, including the switch defense, considered to be a defense with both zone and individual defensive principles. Offenses were forced to expand their base as each defense encountered meant a different type offense to counter these three distinct defenses.

Until the end of World War II, basketball was more sectionally interpreted by coaches. Most travel was by train or bus, and there were few intersectional trips, especially not coast to coast. The time element precluded long-distance travel. Athletes couldn't miss classes the long train rides would entail. Ned Irish, head of Madison Square Garden, convened our first intersectional rivalry by scheduling double headers played several times a week in the Garden during the mid-1930s. To help finance the high cost of air travel, a three-game trip was added that included a game in Buffalo and one in both Philadelphia and New York. Usually four days were spent in playing the three games. This program had a tremendous impact on the standardization of the game. Basketball owes a lot to Ned Irish and his trusted and more-than-able assistant, John Goldner. They contributed much to standardizing the rules interpretations and also gave the game a national aura, showing the world how exciting the game had become. For a coach or a college player, playing a game in Madison Square Garden was the equivalent of an actor playing on Broadway.

One of the early principal problem basketball encountered was breaking down the sectional concepts of the game. In the East, an offensive screen was more closely called than in any other sector. It was difficult for schools from outside the eastern area to adjust to this close interpretation. Conversely, traveling violations were very loosely called, and this made defense more difficult to play. These are but two examples of many differences in rules interpretations that existed then and, to a lesser extent, through the 1950s.

One of the responsibilities coaches felt at that time was that the game of basketball was their game, and thus their responsibility was to guide it through its early growth. I volunteered to try to develop a film that would detail those differences in how rules were interpreted. It had never been done, as the referees' association opposed the creation of such a film. Frankly, I said, "To hell with them. If it could help create a national game with common interpretations of the rules, everyone, including the officials, would benefit—but the biggest benefit will be the consistency of the officiating of our game."

I must detail the monster I created. With the help of Rene Hererrias, my assistant at Cal in 1957, and my film man who lent me his studio, I began my campaign. I wrote to more than 100 coaches in all sections of the country for film showing interpretations of traveling, screening, defensive position, and many such situations. I was deluged with film; most of it showing how the coach got jobbed by an official. Many comical situations also were captured on film, for example. Two officials (only two worked a game at that time) colliding on the sideline as one took the wrong path on transition and then a sudden interception. They wanted to call a foul on each other, as they both became angry. In spite of these types of occurrences and other unimaginable film we received, we managed to make a decent do-it-yourself film on the inconsistencies of rules interpretation by the various conferences and their head officials. I would speculate that both Rene and I spent more than 100 hours in the spring and early summer putting the film together so that it was presentable and factual. Once the leading officials and those heads of conferences saw the film, they realized it was not an official-bashing film but an honest effort to bring about a needed standardization of rules interpretations throughout our basketball world. I was pleased to see that a really professional film was introduced the next year by those people who had originally opposed the concept. As a result, films are now a major contributor to the betterment of officiating and interpretation of new rules.

Soon after World War II, changes in the game emerged, both offensively and defensively. More creativity of offense was noticeable, and the inversion concept stimulated the thinking of many coaches. However, the defensive changes and newer concepts were even more widespread. The press defense in its many forms became very popular in the 1950s. Fast-break coaches liked the stimulus it gave to their up-tempo game. Transition offense became more of a weapon and began to be a part of many coaches' offensive thinking. The skill and athletic level of the individual players increased as the game became more popular at the lower levels of basketball play.

Defenses had to find ways to counter with the various offensive weapons caused by the rule changes that were instituted in the late '30s. Slowly, the defenses met the challenge. Coaches conceived the various concept zones and zone presses—e.g. 1-3-1, 2-3, 3-2, and 1-2-2. Press defenses—full court, three-quarter court and half court—were also developed. Sideline traps, as well as the standard corner traps, also present problems with which an offense has to deal. Assigned-individual defenses became somewhat like an amoeba—different looks but basically the same. Switch defenses were not as widely accepted in total forms, but their strengths were often incorporated in zones and the assigned individual defense, which was a reverse of the switch thinking in the '30s.

In the late 1940s, half-court assigned-individual stat defenses were for the most part one-dimensional defenses, especially in the East and parts of the South and Midwest. The defensive individual had one responsibility, and that was to stop the assigned opponent. Vision was solely on the assigned offensive player. Midpoint vision and communication were not a part of defensive teachings. Weakside defenders were not encumbered by post-help responsibilities. Switching was not permitted as a defender denied off the ball strongly, and off the ball, the defender was always alert for a weakside cut to the ball. As a result, defensive post play was usually behind the post player as fronting was dangerous because of lack of weakside help.

Conversely, in the West we grew up with the weakside slough, midpoint vision and the team concept. We were tough on defense but unimaginative and behind the game offensively. We were more conscious of a defensive rebounder screening his opponent than of his clearing the rebound and initiating a break. Frankly, I loved to play half-court basketball with the East teams, as our offense was best suited to attack the no-help, vision-on-opponent-only type defense. However, we needed to be more conscious of defending the fast-break when we met teams from other sectors. When John Wooden came to UCLA in the late '40s, he brought the Piggy Lambert (the great Purdue coach) type running offense for which the Midwest was famous. John had played for Piggy and Purdue and had grown up with Indiana up-tempo basketball. He also brought an offensive concept that I termed, for want of a better description, "the spread-court offense." We would call it transition offense today. His players had the green light to shoot whenever they felt they were open and in range. It was a real departure from what we were exposed to as players, because an inviolable rule was never to shoot unless offensive rebounders were in place. I believe John learned a lot of his defensive concepts from us, and I know we learned offensive concepts from John. We, as a result, had a faster-type tempo game that was more exciting. As coaches, we all borrow ideas and styles of play from one another. Dr. Naismith invented the game. In spite of what some coaches think, the rest of us borrow and try to better refine it.

The assigned-individual defense has stood the test of time. It has been bent at times but never broken. Its success rests in its ability to incorporate zone principles without compromising its individual mental and physical requirements. It is able to take the best attributes of a switch defense and still maintain its aggressiveness and individual responsibilities. It can meet the ball beyond the perimeter if needed, or slough back to a point inside the perimeter. It can double at the wing with a guard and forward in a crossing situation and attempt to close the outlet pass with the other three defenders. It can create problems that a zone defense presents with alert, aggressive weakside help. In short, an assigned-individual team defense can take on many forms as it incorporates the strengths of a zone defense and the switch principles without losing its integrity of aggressiveness, intensity, determination, proper vision and communication.

Defenses get their greatest test when rule changes are enacted. The change in the screen rule in the late '60s certainly tested the weakside defender playing an aggressive on-the-defender screen and trying simultaneously to deny the offensive opponent. Some coaches simply switched this weakside screen to avoid a possible foul or an unopposed open shot. The impact of the 3-point shot became more of a defensive problem than an offensive worry. Basic transition defense historically retreated to the paint area and adjusted out from the paint. It was soon apparent that an accurate 3-point shooter could seldom be guarded on transition if the back defender had more than one foot in the paint. The quickness of the sideline pass to a 3-point shooter made it difficult to defend or even to bother a wing player set up at the perimeter or the sideline for the 3-point shot.

It is important for coaches to examine new rules, especially those with a real potential immediate impact. Coaches should try to be flexible enough in their basic concept of team defense in order to make whatever adjustment is necessary to counter these new rules and their demands. Whether a coach agrees with a new rule is really unimportant, but making it work for the coach and his/her team is important.

CHAPTER 3

ASSIGNED INDIVIDUAL DEFENSE

PHYSICAL ASPECTS OF INDIVIDUAL DEFENSE

Position

Defensive position in basketball when defending the ball basically relates to foot position and stance. This position should be between the ball handler and the basket being defended. Naturally, instances occur of an overplay to one side or the other. These overplays are predetermined positions that the coach demands in certain situations. Also, overplays are often the result of a vocal call of a teammate to inform that this teammate is in a help situation. A slight move to the side away from the "help" call will reduce the effectiveness and threat of a drive to the basket. An overplay on one side and help on the other side will discourage most offensive players from challenging the defense.

The initial position of the defender is very important but must be accompanied by a maintenance of the position between the ball and the basket. Lateral movement of the defender's feet will deter an offensive driver from forcing a drive and can create an offensive foul or charge. In the lateral defensive slide, the balance can be sustained only by proper hand and arm use. If the inside hand is used as the defender slides laterally with this offensive drive, two positives can happen, and often do. The defender will maintain his or her fundamental position and by the use of the inside hand and forearm pressure, if necessary, can alter the path of the driver. Forearm pressure is used to counter-balance an offensive driver from physically forcing a direct path to the basket. A defensive player by rule is allowed his or her defensive position (a defender's arms can be held in a position parallel to the floor).

Maintaining position off the ball is a necessity for good team play. Vision and proper position off the ball are closely related. A simple rule of off-the-ball backline defense is that as the ball is advanced to the weakside, the movement of this backline weakside defender is toward the ball and slightly backward. The backward movement will help ensure peripheral vision of the offensive player and the ball. The farther away the ball is dictates how far away from the offensive player and how far back to maintain ball and player vision. In the situation that has been described, the responsibility of a weakside backline defender must relate to the post help with which the defender is charged. Should the ball be advanced to the wing on the opposite side of the court, back help must be tempered by a responsibility to beat a cut by the opponent to whom the defender is assigned or a cross court pass from wing to wing.

I believe that the most difficult position to defend effectively is a backline, weakside offensive player when the ball is on the opposite wing. Peripheral vision is very difficult if the offensive player moves to the vicinity of the baseline. Should vision only on the ball occur, a back cut is difficult to defend. Should vision encompass only the assigned opponent, a back screen by the offensive post man could free the offensive player for a close-in shot.

An offense that was widely accepted in the late '40s through the '60s was reverse action. In this pattern, the weakside vision and position problem was a focal point of its success. The Chicago Bulls were very successful employing this screen and cut or back cut in their successful triple-post offense when winning championships in the '90s.

We often wonder why coaches don't build offensive sets on the difficulty of defending certain situations. We all borrow from each other, but some refine and teach better than others. If a coach has flexibility within his or her theoretical concepts of the game, the need for expanding this theoretical base will allow for the adoption of new ideas that will conform within the parameters of this theoretical base. Too many coaches become cloistered and wedded to a system of play that often denies new approaches. This cloistered thinking can be the downfall for a coach and career. Resisting new concepts that are made necessary because of rules changes and or a particular type of team personnel can be very ucounterproductive. As a result, coaches must accept the fact that the game of basketball is a game of change as it adjusts to these new rules, new concepts of play and, as has been previously mentioned, better-skilled or lesser-skilled personnel. Simply stated, coaches must be flexible enough in thought so that there is room for embracing new ideas that could be successful.

Stance

The game of basketball has been described in numerous ways by many people. The description that is most often voiced or written is that "basketball is a game of habit." It is a game that demands quick mental and physical adjustments; it's a game that demands quick, intuitive-type reactions, as well as being a game of body balance, physical quickness, foot skills and ability. It's a game in which the average player must expect to handle the ball 10 percent of the game, and, yet the player must use his or her feet 100 percent of the time while the player is in the game. Players must learn to play both with the ball and without it. In most instances, they must expect to play half the game on defense.

There are many descriptions of what constitutes a physical habit. My definition is that a habit is a conditioned reflex inculcated by a repetitive physical act. It can't be initiated by a piece of chalk nor by just spoken words, regardless of the tone of the spoken words. The theory of contradiction tells us we that can't sit and stand at the same time, nor can we have contradictory habits for the same physical act. If this theory is to be accepted, we cannot expect to change a habit of vision and physical stance by words or chalk. Also, the conditioned mental reactions to situations may be compromised if during a time-out the coach demands a change of physical and mental play that will create these contradictions. Granted, this is arguable, but the logic is difficult to refute.

How does a coach create the proper fundamental physical position of a basketball player? The proper fundamental position that basketball playing demands is in contradiction to what every physically-able human accepts as normal. The normal stance we all assume when standing is a straight-legged upright stance; yet we as coaches constantly exhort our players to assume a low, flexed-knee, comfortably-based stance. Can we expect just by a verbal demand that the player will change his or her normal physical stance because the coach vocally demands it? A momentary reaction by the player from his or her normal stance to the proper basketball stance may result, but habit will prevail soon afterward and the player will again be stiff-legged. What is the answer?

If we are to accept the need of a proper, physical act to enhance the ability of a player to consistently maintain the appropriate defensive stance, the player must be put in a physical drill that is repetitive, physically correct, and demanding. It should be an important part of the early-season conditioning drills and a part of the daily practice plan. The "hands-up drill" was formulated earlier in my coaching career while searching for an answer to the stance problem. It seemed logical to me that since a basketball player plays 90 percent of the time without the ball, coaches should institute drills that were complementary to a basketball player's total efficiency when he or she is not in possession of the ball.

This drill has many purposes, including:

- to condition and strengthen the calves and upper legs that support the body in the low, flexed-knee stance
- to strengthen the support muscles that enable players to raise their arms defensively and not be physically affected in their shooting because of tired arms
- to increase the stamina and endurance of players as the time demands of the drill increase each day
- to strengthen the will and commitment of players as they fight the urge to give in to the increasing physical demands of this drill
- to have players gain respect for their teammates as each player has endured similar pain; thus the demand to "gut it out" will be created

Upon examination, the relevance of those objectives is fairly obvious, including the following:

- When a player engages in a drill, a physical habit is being conditioned. For example, to maintain their defensive stance for the duration of the game, the players must strengthen the muscles involved in supporting this stance. These muscles can best be strengthened by a physical drill that involves these muscles. Each day the time span of the drill should be increased in order to increase the stamina and endurance level of the muscles involved.

- There is a boxing axiom that holds true for defensive basketball. "When the legs stiffen, the arms drop and the beating begins." A flexed-knee player will have a clear step on a stiff-legged opponent. How often do coaches vocally remind their players on defense to raise a hand in a shooter's face, if only to lessen the shooter's concentration on his or her shot.

- How often are games won because of one's team's superior conditioning over the opponent? How often do we see one team end the first half with a splurge of points that eventually prove to be the winning margin? The same is frequently true in the last five minutes of a game. An NCAA tournament winner was determined when a retreating player gave in to tiredness and allowed a player to be open up court for an easy shot. A defensive teammate had to leave the basket area open in order to challenge the open player, but to no avail. It happens far too often, as we know. The drill creates the will not to give in to fatigue. In so doing, the drill establishes a situation where lesser-conditioned opponents are retreating at half speed or not filling wings on a potential fast break situation for their teams. As the drill builds the physical support, it also steels the will not to give in. Players are being taught to reach down for more energy.

- The Marine Corps has a slogan: "If you can do 20 pushups, do 21." This catch phrase simply implies, "Shoot above the mark, and you will usually hit it. Aim only at the mark, and you will often be below it." Each day the physical demands imposed by the drill are increased by a minute or two minutes until a maximum duration is reached. A maximum for a college team should not exceed 20 minutes; for high schoolers, 12 minutes. The initial drill should be two minutes for high school and four minutes for the college player. The front foot should be changed once each drill and at the halfway mark, i.e., for high schoolers, one minute right foot forward, change to left foot for one minute; for college, two minutes right foot, two minutes left foot. No time lapse should be allowed as the front foot changes.

Every coach wants team unity—mutual respect among players and between players and coach. Successful teams are teams that have had a vigorous, demanding conditioning program that tests the will of each player. I would imagine the highest accolade a player could receive from his teammates is "There is a person I would go to war with." Defense demands this interdependence (respect of each for the other). Drills that enhance these qualities should be a part of a team's early training and conditioning process.

Ambidexterity of the feet has the same importance as hand ambidexterity. A right-handed player often only relies on the right foot for the initiation of a drive to the basket, and this lessens his or her total offensive game. Players should be put through drills that will create a dependence on either foot when initiating movement. Such drills permit, and even demand, the exercise and conditioning of the weaker foot to the same degree as thenaturally dominant foot, the right foot. The reverse is true for a left-handed and left-footed player.

By changing the commands of each movement forward, backward or laterally, a player will be conditioned to move equally well with either foot as the player experiences the drill each day. Hakeem Olajuwan is often praised as having the best footwork ever of any center in the NBA. Anyone seeing this remarkable athlete execute his many foot skills has to be impressed. When asked how he developed his remarkable footwork, his answer was his early years of playing soccer, years before he ever played basketball. The demands of ambidexterity of the feet in soccer cause the player to constantly practice on the weaker foot—for passing and dribbling (soccer style), the protection of the ball, and finally for shooting with either foot. A real similarity exists in basketball for similar demands on foot ambidexterity, since a player who can take a strong first step only with the right foot, will soon experience an overplay on the right foot by the defense.

Mechanics of the Hands-Up Drill

- Spread team members in rows spaced about six feet across, four to a row, with spacing between rows of 6-to-8 feet. For a squad of 12 players, three rows of four players should be employed.

- Players assume a defensive stance—knees flexed, right hand up and right foot forward.

- When the coach calls "change feet" at the midpoint of the drill (after three minutes if the total time planned for the drill is six minutes, as an example), the change is immediate. Players must keep their designated foot forward until they hear "change feet."

- A voice command carries more authority than a hand signal. As the players tire, a louder, more urging voice gets better response from the players. If the coach is hoarse after several days of the drill, the coach is doing a good job.

- The commands are forward, rear, right, and left. The cadence varies so that there is no anticipation of commands. Different cadences should be used as the length of the drill increases; it adds spice, since the drill can become boring as well as tiring.

- This is a pre-season, conditioning drill that should not be used during the season or just prior to the first game. The physical demands on the players' leg muscles have a tendency to deaden the legs while they are strengthening them. Players will not shoot as accurately as they normally would, as the initial lift will be affected. While leg fatigue can be a by-product of a sound conditioning program, strengthening the musculature of the legs is a critical goal. Because it is pre-season, games are not a problem or a priority—nor should they be.

In the process, a coach helps to prepare a team for the competitive schedule by enhancing the following:

- conditioning
- organization of offense and defense with breakdown part-method drills
- refinement of the defense, the offense, and special situations, e.g., out-of-bounds plays, jump balls, pregame drills, etc.

Coaches cannot expect well-conditioned teams if they start with refinement and ignore early organization. Because teaching and conditioning pre-season practice varies at the high school level, the time allotted for each phase has to be proportionally spaced. Sometimes refinement does not come in the early stages of the early practice games. Because variances exist due to facilities and other factors at the college level, common sense dictates that time be spent on each phase, but the order should not be changed.

Again to borrow an axiom from another sport—golf: "You drive for show and you putt for dough." In basketball, the December non-league games are the driving for show. The March games, putting for dough. No one ever won a league, conference, state title or NCAA championship in December. These are won normally in March—a few instances in late February, the NCAA in late March or early April.

The basic purpose of explaining the hands-up drill in such detail is not to sell you on this particular drill but to have you create your own conditioning drills with these specific objectives in mind. When drills demand a great physical commitment on the part of the players, it is not to punish them physically but to make them understand more thoroughly what is physically expected of them if they are to be conditioned to properly compete.

One coach may not have the same ability as his or her opponent, nor the experience or wisdom of the other coach; one's facilities might pale in comparison with those of the opposing school, but there is no excuse for having less well-conditioned players than the opponent. All coaches should keep in mind that everyone starts even in this regard.

Vision

One of the most important fundamentals of good individual and team defense is vision. Proper vision and defensive position are the chief contributing factors to the success of a team's defense. "Peripheral" and "midpoint" are the most popular designations given by the coach in describing vision in basketball.

One of the most important rules of vision is moving back and slightly toward the ball as the opponents move the ball on the perimeter toward the opposite wing. Every time the ball moves, both vision and position should change. As the ball moves away, the defender's stance should open, and as the ball advances towards the defender, the defender's inside foot and stance should commence closing. The purpose of the movement back and away is to ensure midpoint vision and, by opening the stance as the ball moves away, defender is positioned to quickly help the post-up player with position and vocal help.

Situations exist in which a defender must make a decision visually. Should the vision go to the opponent or to the ball? I contend that it should go to the ball. If this decision is made, the midpoint of vision should go from ball to midpoint, not midpoint to ball. As the defender goes to the ball vision, he or she should extend the arms back and away to overplay a back cut possibility and try to "feel" the opponent who is out of the defender's vision. Often the touch alone will help re-establish midpoint vision.

Some defenders are head turners. They turn their eyes from the ball to their opponent and back to the ball. Smart offensive players will backcut the head turners. When the vision encompasses only the opponent, a back screen will often be the answer by the offense. With peripheral vision, a side screen and most back screens can be anticipated. Also, a backcut can be defended when midpoint vision is used. Proper vision is never more tested than when the defender is playing the opponent off the ball.

While the team defense has many component parts, none is more important than vision—peripheral vision. The "why" of this factor needs to be communicated to team members. The "why" has many reasons for its importance. When a weakside defender with midpoint vision sees a loose ball recovery as an interception by a teammate, the ability of this weakside defender to convert immediately to offense will often result in an easy basket. Because this defender is facing the basket downcourt and the opponent the defender is covering is facing the near basket, the converting defender will usually have a step or more as he or she races upcourt for a potential pass. Most teams are more dangerous in this type of transition than they are in their fast break. Seldom will an easy transition basket occur in this circumstance if the weakside vision encompasses only an opponent. Players will more readily accept midpoint vision if they see the benefit an alert, properly-visioned defender receives.

Do's of Vision

- Proper vision can help teammates when they lose their opponent and must depend on help to pick up the loose, open opponent.
- The quickness of a basket after a forced turnover has created a favorable transition situation. It can be a lone, alert defender breaking free to an open basket or teammates quickly converting and having numbers—2-on-3 or 3-on-4—on the opponents.
- The quickness of reaction to a loose-ball recovery and a gaining-ball possession creates a positive feeling and a negative reaction by the player and the team that lost the ball. Without ball vision, the loose ball recovery will not ensue.

Don'ts of Vision

- Don't watch your opponent's eyes when defending your opponent with the ball. Concentrate your vision on the torso or stomach area of your opponent.

- Don't watch your opponent's feet. A defender will be susceptible to a shot or a pass. Foot fakes are the tools of a good offensive player, and a defender can be mesmerized by an explosive step, a crossover, a rocker step or a simple foot fake.

- Don't watch the ball directly. Your midpoint between the feet and the head is the trunk of the opponent. The trunk of a basketball player follows movement; it doesn't initiate it.

- Don't forget to be like the kid who takes the basketball to the playground. If the kid doesn't keep an eye on the ball, he or she will probably go home without it.

Communication

Successful defensive play has many component parts. It is difficult for me even to imagine a good defensive unit that does not communicate. Simple communication on a basketball court is relaying information to help each teammate to defend better. It will signal the possibilities of various offensive screens and or backside help to a teammate trying to defend a post player, a front line teammate engaged in playing the ball, and the myriad situations that occur over the course of the game.

Communication should first start when the defense picks up the ball. As simple as that may seem, this evolving situation creates as many defensive breakdowns as any single occurrence on the court defensively. Sometimes, the ball will be progressing downcourt with two defenders positioned to pick up the ball. Sometimes neither picks up the ball, sometimes both. Each instance is attributable to no vocal call. Both players should be ready to call "ball" as the ball progresses toward them. Whoever calls first takes the ball, while the second defender backs off to pick up an open opponent.

How often do we see a situation where both defenders pick up the ball and allow an open opponent a pass and an uncontested shot? The most important opponent to defend is the one with the ball. He or she must be defended, but normally not by two defenders. This simple problem can be corrected by drills that reenact this game situation. It must become a defensive habit.

Many centuries ago, a Chinese philosopher, Confucius, stated that "a picture is worth a thousand words." By the same token, this age-old adage can be applied to basketball by saying, "a word in basketball can give many pictures." Take for example the word "empty." Coaches should always try to get single words to describe quickly the situations that may occur. Short, concise descriptive words are the answer. In a situation in which the frontline defender is playing the ball, presumably with help behind at the wing, this position will be between the basket and the ball with a slight overplay away from the backside help. The backside help suddenly must defend a backcut and vacate the wing area. The only way the frontline defender who is occupied defending the ball handler can know if there is backside help is a vocal call by the backline defender. The loud call of "empty" results from this back-door cut. When the call "empty" is heard, the defender on the ball then overplays to the side of the call, as that is now an open and vulnerable side. Likewise, the weakside defenders should move several steps to this now-open side. Because the weakside is occupied by an extra defender at this point, these defender teammates have the benefit of an extra defender who can vocally help them if they are backcut to the open side. The overplay of the defender on the ball reduces the effectiveness of the offensive ball handler taking advantage of this open side. Without communication, it would be difficult to feel a sense of security when playing frontline defense on the ball.

Communication by a defensive post player is extremely important. If the offensive post player is stationed at a high post, a "high post" call should be made. It indicates that the immediate basket area is relatively open for a back cut, a post pass and a baseline cut by the passer, a one-on-one drive by a wing player going baseline, a weakside slicing to the basket. A call of "low post" indicates the vulnerability to a drive over the top or a pass and fake baseline and then cutting over the top without the ball, the front line being aware that they must "slough off" a little extra distance to narrow this vulnerable passing lane between the low post and the frontline defenders.

When the post player is being fronted by the post defender, this defender must rely on the vocal call of "help here" by the backline help defender. With this help, the defender can better defend the post player. If, however, "empty" is called from the backline helper, the defender must now readjust the defensive post position to lessen the effectiveness of an over-the-top lob pass. In this instance, the front can become a high side position by the defensive post player. Again, when a defender is playing the ball or trying to defend a post player without the ball, good, loud communication is absolutely necessary.

The player guarding the ball should always hear where the help is. "Help here" is a common call to the ball defender by the immediate teammates. Furthermore, communication psychologically gives each defender a positive feeling of teammates helping each other.

Summary—Communication
Sound communication can enhance defensive play in a number of ways, including:
- Enables defender to pick up the ball
- Assures the ball defender of help positions
- Strengthens each individual defender's confidence in his/her support
- Allows for more aggressive defensive on-ball play
- Emphasizes importance of the "we" and "us" of defense

Each element of the physical aspects of defensive basketball is important. A defender can be positioned properly, but without the communication of the defensive teammates, this defender will defend with less confidence and aggressiveness because he or she will have no idea of where the help defense is or isn't. The importance of mid-point or peripheral vision can never be underestimated, yet its importance is lessened if the defender on and off the ball loses the defensive position associated with fundamental defense. Communication loses its importance if the defender communicating loses position on the assigned opponent and forgets the importance of ball-encompassing vision. Initial position is very important, but maintaining this position as the ball or the assigned opponent moves is equally important. Successful defensive teams are those that combine all of the essential elements for sound individual defense to make strong individual defenders into an efficient and effective team defense.

MENTAL REQUIREMENTS OF INDIVIDUAL DEFENSE

Too often coaches neglect the importance of the mental requirements needed for a productive, competitive, assigned-individual defense. The physical aspects may be letter perfect, but if the mental aspects are missing, it will be ineffectual. However, without the proper physical mechanics to blend with these mental requirements, the defense would be inconsistent and unproductive. Among the critical mental basics that lend themselves to an effective assigned-individual defense are the following:

Aggressiveness

Controlled aggressiveness is another common trait of successful defensive teams. Aggressiveness and alertness are common allies in playing defense. A strength of the assigned-individual defense is the ability to detail the individual responsibilities of each defensive player. There are no vague areas. The potential for competitive stimulation can create a more competitive level of interest as the coach details each opposing player's strengths and weaknesses. Coaches must understand that the emotional and aggressive state of mind this type defense can create is sometimes compromised by a change to a more passive, less-aggressive type defense. Emotions are not like tap water that can be turned on and off. A coach may run the risk of losing a really aggressive competitive edge if the player has to reduce aggressiveness because of a defensive change.

Alertness

The mental contributions to an effective defense are many, not the least of which is alertness. The reaction to loose balls, careless, telegraphed passes and unexpected happenings are but some of the positives an alert defender gives his or her team. Often, one alert player can be used as an example of what the player is giving to the team.

Determination

The effective defender takes the challenge of shutting down the assigned opponent with a determination and resolve that often says, "this opponent is not going to beat us." Five defenders with this same same level of determination to shut down their assigned opponents can create a team resolve that makes the defender's team tough to defeat. Usually, the really determined defender puts on a game face well before the game begins. It can become contagious to the rest of the team.

Initiative

I have yet to see a really good defender who didn't have defensive initiative. There is no rule in the book that states that the defensive player must always react to the offensive player's fakes. A good defender will initiate the faking and cause the offensive player to react to the defender's fakes. Initiative defensively is simply having the offensive player reacting to the defensive player. While the advantage may be slight, it gives the defender, rather than the offensive player, an edge. A slow-footed offensive player can beat a much quicker defender with good foot skills because the offensive player knows what is being set up. However, this same slow-footed player who is now on defense must rely on the appropriate mental basics to have any chance of defending a quicker offensive opponent.

Anticipation

There is an old basketball adage that best refers to individual defense: "Play the opponents off the ball with alert, aggressive denial, and they will be easier to defend when they get the ball." Spacing is, in most instances, the single most important part of offensive play. Allowing opponents to operate in their familiar spacing areas will cause an offense to function much better than if they are forced out of their normal spacing. Anticipating passes from a guard to a wing player will often force the opponent out of the normal spacing, thus having to receive the pass well out of the normal wing area. This wing opponent with the ball can often be played loosely. Forcing the wing opponent out of the normal spacing means that passes are longer into the basket area, which increases the interception risk. A flat pass to an outside guard is more likely to be intercepted. Similarly, such a pass may force the offensive outside guard to move well back toward the midline to protect the pass. This type of situation takes the fluidity and normal movement away from the offense as the spacing is distorted. Furthermore, this loose defensive play on the wing player lessens the effectiveness of this offensive wing player in trying to drive the ball to the basket.

Competitiveness

Players like to compete. Coaches want their team to compete. The assigned-individual defense will bring out the competitiveness of players because they know their responsibilities in stopping the assigned opponents. Competing isn't about getting beaten on a single play but adjusting and making the assigned adjustment and change. It's not about making a spectacular play occasionally but about being a consistent, steady defender who is capable of understanding and adjusting his or her play as needed.

Summary—Mental Requirements of Individual Defense

It is important that the coach realizes that, in teaching individual defense, the emphasis cannot be solely upon the physical demands of individual defensive play. Drills must be incorporated into daily practice plans that stress the many mental requirements of solid, successful individual and team defensive play.

As described in the physical requirements section, productive defense, both individually and teamwise, must be a blend of all the physical requirements. Yet, blending these requirements without a recognition of the importance of the mental basics would fall short of what could be accomplished defensively. A defender could have fundamental position, proper vision, be helped by good support communication, and yet not be nearly as effective as he or she could be. Mental alertness and those other elements of the mental requirements are signifying features of a good defender and an excellent defensive team.

How does a coach instill these important elements of superior defensive play? Again, it is teaching through the use of drills that encompass these qualities of defense. I don't believe a coach can get satisfactory results by merely vocally exhorting or demanding these qualities of play. Only by patient teaching, carefully explaining "why" these qualities are important, and performing numerous repetitions of these drills will these defensive requirements become a habit. Those coaches who believe in the part-method or breakdown teaching will be rewarded by their players not only knowing how to defend but also knowing the "why" of their defense.

INDIVIDUAL ASSIGNED DEFENSE

Individual Defense on the Ball

Spacing is probably the single most important facet of offensive basketball. Good spacing allows for proper distance and angles of the pass. If spacing is such an important aspect of offense, then the individual defender should realize the importance of denying easy entries and, by the denial, hopefully distort passing angles and distances by forcing the receiving opponent out of his or her normal spacing. A fundamental truism in basketball is: a player must first have the ball before the player can score a point. It would then be wise to approach individual defense in this manner. The defender should play the opponent aggressively and be conscious of the importance of this denial. Too many players feel that individual defense begins when the offensive assigned opponent receives the ball. Actually, individual defense is more productive and effective when the defender plays an aggressive denial defense thereby forcing the opponent farther from the basket, which will probably reduce the effective shooting area by 10 or more percent. If this is the case, the offensive player is less likely to shoot, so a slight backoff by the defender would be in order. This slight backoff creates more passing and driving problems for the offensive player. Frontline defensive responsibilities are different from backline responsibilities. Coaches should be aware of and understand the differences and the importance of each.

Backline Responsibilities—Playing the Defensive Wing Position

The importance of forcing the receiving opponents out of their normal operational zones or wing spacing has previously been discussed. The defensive wing player should play the opponent tightly, slightly on top with the inside foot extended. The stance must be low with the inside hand extended and parallel to the floor. The back hand should be positioned in an extended manner but not as high as the other arm. This back arm can alert the defender to a back cut as the back hand is in slight contact with the opponent. This defensive position does not have to "body" the opponent. Over-aggressive denial can cause fouls and also be susceptible to a reverse pivot and seal on the defender by the opponent. Defenders should keep daylight and depend on footwork in this position. Furthermore, they should remember that the inside foot is that foot closest to the paint area.

Defending the Ball at the Wing Position

When an offensive wing player receives the ball, the position of the defender should be of utmost importance. When the defender is positioned straight up in the one-on-one confrontation, the inside foot should be the extended foot, the inside hand in the opponent's vision line should be close enough to be a distraction but not too close to allow for an easy drive. A low base and flexed knee are absolutely necessary to assure quick movement in any direction. Vision should be at chest level, and there should be a voice call of "ball" as the opponent receives the ball. Why is the inside foot forward? It is a common thought among most coaches that the extended foot is the foot that should be attacked in a one-on-one situation. It would then be reasonable to have the weaker foot extended in the vicinity that the defender has help. The frontline defender should be on the side of the extended foot so help in that direction is more than possible. This initial stance as described is strongest defending a baseline drive. Furthermore, if the communication of the frontside defensive helper is a loud "help here," the defender on the ball takes a slight overplay baseline side or away from the vocal help. This slight overplay takes away a direct straight-line drive opportunity.

In the event of a drive by the offensive player going baseline, the defender should always use the inside hand to best control the driver. The position of this inside hand should be extended and at hip level. With this hand position, the path of the driver can be misdirected from the basket to an angle between the basket and the near side line corner. Even more important is the balance in movement that the defender enjoys as the feet are "crow hopped" but never crossed by the use of this inside hand. Balance is absolutely essential to have body control should the offensive driver suddenly stop for a quick jumper. The importance of the feet and their correct use is never more exemplified than in this situation.

Why shouldn't the defender use the outside hand? Too many times, experience has shown that the outside hand reduces the ability of the defender to maintain position between the ball and the basket. This overuse of the outside hand reduces balance and recovery ability, and a defensive foul is more apt to be called. Violating the rule that an extended arm cannot impede the path of an offensive player with the ball is one of the easiest calls an official will normally have. Overuse of the hands and arms and less dependence on foot movement probably account for more losing seasons than any other single factor. The rule of "feet first, hands second" should be reminded often to team members.

Some coaches prefer to have a stance that is lateral with neither foot forward. The problem with that approach is that a smart player will fake a drive over the top and cause that foot to react, and the defender now is forced to defend the baseline with the baseline foot forward.

When the offensive wing player drives over the top or to the middle, the defender's hand position changes, as does the movement of the feet. The front foot extends in the direction of the driver with the opposite hand, now the left or inside hand, as opposed to a wing player defending a driver going right baseline, the right foot has been forward so the right arm is the inside arm at the hip of the driver. When the drive is to the left or over the top, the left hand at this point is positioned at the hip of the driver, while the right arm and hand are up and away from the ball. Too often in this situation, the right hand extends to impede the driver.

Three things usually happen:

- The defender loses the important lateral movement as balance is being sacrificed.
- The defender is called for a defensive illegal impediment.
- The defender swipes at the ball, misses, and the driver takes it to the hoop— often for a lay-up.

These three negative factors far outweigh the very few times an extended arm creates a turnover.

There are many reasons for maintaining defensive position on a driver. Too often, this individual-style offense creates the necessity for a team rotation that results in a lay-up or an easy offensive rebound basket as most rotating creates a size mismatch on the weak side of the basket. Too much dependence on rotation can be fool's gold, as it supports lazy defenders who rely on teammates to pick up their mistakes. Always remember, offense can be a one-on-one, a two-on-two or a three-on-three. Seldom do we see more than a passer, screener and a cutter directly involved in the creation of a shot. On the other hand, defense cannot be played by fewer than all five players if it is to be played well. It's this interdependence of each defensive player relying on his or her teammates that validates a strong defense. As has been pointed out, one lazy defender, individually playing, can break down a team defense. Rotation is the best hope, and probably the only hope, for the defense with defenders playing individual defense, not team defense.

Frontline Individual Defense on the Ball

It is extremely important for a ballside, frontline defender to be positioned, initially, above the normal perimeter of the team defense as the ball is being traversed over the midline. This extended position can often cause the opponent's offense to be directed to the sideline and away from their spacing. A rule of good half-court defense is to try to make the opponent start his or her offense from a standing position—if possible, from a standing position not related to the team's normal spacing. By meeting the ball slightly behind the midcourt line and in a slightly restrictive stance, this can often happen.

Should the ball be picked up out of the normal operational area, deflections and interceptions are often caused because of poor passing angles and distorted distances. Sometimes the defender on the ball can create real problems to the ball handler if immediate on-ball pressure is exerted on the ball handler as the ball is picked up.

The basic position of a frontline defender is between the ball and the basket. Because of the point value of the 3-point shot, the ball must have more pressure than it did prior to the 3-point shot. This basic defensive position is also conditioned by the vocal help of teammates. If the backline strongside defender shouts "empty" (or whatever voice call a coach uses to signify lack of back help), an overplay to the sideline and the area from where the call came is necessary. Any called backscreen should be loud and clear. An effective backscreen can be a difficult maneuver to defend. A switch is sometimes necessary if the backscreen is well set. If the cutter veers to the side in the 3-point area, the back defender must vacate the basket area to pick up their open player. If this happens, the screener now has a favorable position on the player screened. If this screener seals the player screened, an easy basket can be the result, or the basket area could be open for an easy pass. Defensively, the screened player must quickly move inside or to the paint area and quickly establish a side or behind position on the original screener. A slow readjustment by the screened player of a switch could result in an easy basket. Should the ball be in the hands of a post-up player, backscreens on the weakside can be difficult to defend if clearly explained responsibilities have not been given to the defensive players.

Rules of On-the-Ball Defense

- Pick up the ball as soon as possible, communicating "BALL."
- Pressure the ball everywhere.
- Be fundamentally correct on hand and foot position.
- Be mentally alert for vocal help from teammates.
- Recognize the importance of communication as to your position on the ball.
- Don't underestimate the importance of post communication in regards to positioning on the ball.
- When playing the ball in an isolation instance, recognize the strength of the opponent and the tendencies to setting up the shot.
- In playing the ball away from the basket area, recognize the position of the ball as it relates to the basket and the range and proficiency of your opponent's outside shooting ability.
- Try not to allow your opponent to create space between you and the ball within shooting range.
- Get a hand in the shooter's face prior to the shot.

Playing Defense Off the Ball

Backline defense off the ball can be the most difficult of the defensive positions to play. A wing defender on the ballside has the responsibility of denying the offensive wing player the ball. The primary responsibility of this wing defender is to force the offensive opponent out of the normal wing spacing. While trying to effect a successful denial, the backdoor counter is a constant reminder to the defender not to overcommit in this denial of the ball.

The responsibility of the backline, weakside defender is a very difficult position on defense when the ball is at the foul line extended or the wing position on the opposite side of the floor. The defender will have a vision problem if the offensive player walks the defender to the vicinity of the baseline. Peripheral vision can be compromised, as midpoint vision is difficult. Further, this weakside defender is charged with weakside support for the defensive post player. Defending a back-cut possibility, a fake baseline line cut and then a cut off a center's weakside screen are but some of the problems facing this backline, weakside defender.

The offensive wing player can take three potential paths. A good fake or series of fakes to break clear for the reception of the guard-to-wing pass in the normal wing spacing. Another path is a quick cut to the foul line or a back cut to the opposite side when the ball has been passed to the opposite wing. It's one more reason to validate the thinking of many that the forward or wing position is the most difficult position to properly play in basketball.

Frontline, off-the-ball defense is a situation more of team support and less of individual responsibility. Whenever a defender is not charged with the responsibility of playing the ball handler, the defender is more team defending and helping. Vision and communication come more into play by the off-the-ball defenders.

Screens should normally be called by back defenders. They should be defined as to the responsibilities of the player screened and the defender whose assigned opponent is the screener. Backscreens, in particular, must be anticipated by the back defender, who vocally alerts the teammate who is being screened. Rules pertaining to screens and the responsibilities of the defender involved should be clearly defined. No gray areas should exist if at all possible. Poor communication, slow readjustment and indecision as to the responsibilities of the defender will break down the confidence of the team defense. This is an area in which part-method teaching is of supreme importance.

Rules of Off-the-Ball Defense

- Realize the importance of helping the defender playing the ball.
- Understand that proper off-the-ball vision and position are closely related.
- Be fully aware of the extreme importance of communication (e.g., signaling help vocally, lack of help or "empty" offensive post positions, picking up call with a vocal call, etc.).
- When vision of the ball and the opponent cannot be employed, direct your vision from midpoint to ball, not midpoint to opponent. The ball should have prime importance.
- Charge the off-ball defender with communication of calling screens and the switch, if necessary.
- Don't overextend toward the ball when playing a weakside wing player, as a crosscourt pass from wing-to-wing or a screen preventing a quick adjustment can result. The 3-point shot potential has caused movement   defensively as it relates to the off-the-ball defensive position.

Summary—Individual Defense on the Ball

The use and development of the feet can never be undervalued. A basketball player will play 100 percent of the time with his feet and only 10 percent of the time with the ball. As a result, drills must be incorporated into daily practice plans that help create proper form, movement and balance of the individual defenders on the ball.

POST DEFENSE

As the play of basketball is often transitional basketball, the game has likewise had its many transitions, especially as it has referred to the post game. The 3-second lane in the earlier formative years of basketball has had its arc adjusted from what was initially called the "keyhole" because of the 6-foot, 3-second area and its circle, which resembled a key-hole. This 3-second area has expanded from the initial 6-foot area to its now 12-foot area in the college game and 16 feet in the NBA game. The international game has a totally different configuration with angled lines that extend from the edges of the foul line to the baseline. Its distance at its base is slightly less than 20 feet. The effect of each different marking has had its effect on the type of play of half-court offensive thinking. The history of basketball has shown, time and time again, that major rules changes invoke tactical adjustments of the defense and offense. The change as it applies to the 3-point shot has created more of an emphasis on outside shooting with the purpose of unmassing the defense from defending just the basket area. In turn, this action has generated a need for a rethinking of tactics employed in defending the post man.

Various schools of thought exist regarding defending the post player. Some believe in single coverage; others in doubling the post player with a variance of the second defense player or the doubler, as this player is often called.

Single Coverage

Single coverage is the conventional type of post defense used over the many years of the game. Fundamentally, if the post is low, the defense plays the baseline side. If the ball is with an outside perimeter player, the defender either goes underneath or rolls over the top of the post player and establishes a position on the inside of the post-up player. The principal reason for these positions is to protect the areas where there is little or no help. The defensive post player must rely on help from the outside strongside defensive front-line player. The post defender will try to play the post player as high as possible without actually fronting him. The purpose of this position is to make the angle of the pass from the wing player as far out as possible, which poses a risk of deflection by the strongside outside defender. The roll is over the top should the wing player with the ball pass to the outside guard. The defensive post man reduces the problem of being sealed by the post by adjusting his position to the inside as the ball is received by the guard. The defender should, again, try to force an angle toward the defensive teammate who is playing the strongside wingman. This basic position stays the same should the ball be reversed to the weakside guard and the weakside forward. Among the important factors in effective post defense are:

- Pressuring the passer
- Vocally helping the post defender from the rear
- Relying on foot movement on each movement of the ball

A danger in this type of defense is being caught in a vulnerable, sealed position as the ball is being reversed. It is especially difficult if the weakside offensive forward cuts to the foul line. A slow-reacting defensive post player is vulnerable to a lob-type pass from the forward to the post player in the lane. Well executed, it will always create problems.

Some coaches who feel this vulnerability will reverse positions on the post player. When the ball is on the wing, they defend from the side opposite the baseline side with the siding to the middle. They will lessen the vulnerability to the foul-line forward pass into the basket area. However, when playing the post player on the high side, there is a vulnerability to the post defender being sealed by the post player as the wing player improves the passing angle by a dribble or two toward the baseline. If the post player can retain his seal, he or she will often get a lay-up if the pass is completed.

Fronting the Post Player

Another adage of the game is that an offensive player can't score unless he or she has the ball. In the high school and college game, this type defense is more effective because the weakside help is not restricted by rule. In the NBA the rules of a "no zone" defense restrict the weakside help a post defender can receive.

When using this type of fronting defense, it is extremely important that pressure is put on the passer. A soft defender on the ball will often defeat this type of defense. If the passer is given no pressure or obstruction by the defender, the situation is similar to the prevent defense employed in football—it sounds good but is rarely effective.

Communication is another defensive factor that must be stressed. The weakside backside defender must vocally reassure the post defender of over-the-top pass help. Should the back defender vacate this area and thus not provide backside help, the word "*EMPTY*" must be communicated, since it implies no backside help. The fronting defender can thus adjust the position at either side of the post player should this "*EMPTY*" call occur.

A defensive counter to this vacating of the area by the backside defensive player is help by the defensive guards. If the offensive weakside forward comes to the foulline, the strongside defensive guard can move into the passing lane from the wingman to the foul-line area of reception by the weakside forward. The weakside defensive guard can overplay his or her position and play a zone-type responsibility and close whichever offensive guard receives the wing pass. Sometimes to close the passing lane, the strongside defensive guard has to fall back so far into the passing that the strongside offensive guard may have an easy open shot. The counter is when the weakside defensive guard position is close enough to the strongside offensive guard that the shot can be denied or at least hurried. The purpose of this type of defense is to allow the weakside backline defensive player to assume a position where the defender is able to contest the over-the-top pass to the fronted opposing center. A defense can be varied to help protect the fronting defensive center. To repeat, pressure on the wing passer can make it difficult to resist the pressure and still read the defensive movement of the post defender.

Double-Down Post Defense

The double-down defense has become a popular counter to a talented center. It's particularly effective in the NBA because of the 24-second clock. A defensive strategy that is widely used in the NBA is to exert pressure on the ball handler in the backcourt, hopefully for eight seconds, and direct the ball handler to a corner of the court as he or she proceeds to the midline and forecourt. Another six or seven or more seconds use of the press is exerted to deny normal spacing of the offense. At this point, an entry that has been denied to the wing is now allowed. The post defender allows a low post to be set. This maneuver can take another three to five seconds, which allows the offensive center about six seconds to make his move. As the ball is passed into this low post, the post defender aggressively denies the baseline, while the weakside defensive guard commits himself to the double down, shutting off any movement by the offensive postman to the paint area. Because the offensive post is at a low-post position, the offensive post player's angles of outlet passing are poor, the distances longer than normal, and trying to hit a cutter is difficult because the passing lane is not good for the cutter to receive a pass from the low-post player. Additionally, should the pass be made, the defensive post is positioned to probably block this in-close shot.

The double can also come from the backline defensive man or the strongside front defensive player. In the NBA, they will normally vary the double-down as there is usually little time to read the defense and determine from where the extra pressure is coming. The principal reason for the NBA double-down is to attack the 24-second clock. The defense tries to delay the pass from the wing player to the post player. This delay will reduce the options the post player has—the longer the delay, the fewer the options.

The double-down will be used at the college and high school programs for different reasons and with a different emphasis on time as it relates to the defense and its motives. A double-down can confuse any post player, especially an inexperienced, poor passing player. It is possible to play it immediately to test the opponent's counter and the manner in which they will handle it. It's a defense, as is the change-up defense, that can rotate into the normal man or assigned-player defense or, possibly, a zone, especially a 1-3-1.

Another situation in which it might be used is in the last 12 to 10 seconds of the time-possession clock. Basically, it's a confusion defense that aggressively attacks the post player. Teams and players often show early signs of panic as they near the end of the time-possession clock. This type of defense can, and often does, confuse the opponent. Often, the result is a hurried, forced shot. Psychologically, it can help the defense.

One of the basic tenets of defense is to try to make a lesser player take the shot rather than a team's star player. Because the star player is often in the middle (i.e. the post player), the double-down frequently results in an offenesive play being started by a pass to a lesser-impact player. Percentage-wise, it is usually good defensive strategy.

In my opinion, the offensive abilities of post players have not been fully utilized in these past two or more decades. The post-offense type of play with its spacing, cutting and counter opportunities has been supplanted by the more popular offenses—the motion or passing game, the flex and the triangle concepts. With the increasing popularity of the 3-point shot, more emphasis is being given to the post-type perimeter spacing. Many coaches at every competitive level have little relationship or knowledge of the post offense, so there is a reluctance to adopt it. The three offenses to which I have referred are what many coaches are familiar with as former players. It's another adage: Coach what you know and know what you coach. It's not easy to adopt a style of play that a coach has little or no working knowledge of. It could be noted, however, that the motion offense was relatively unknown until the rules committee changed the screen rule and its interpretation from what was called the 3-foot rule. This original rule established the legal position of the offensive player to be three feet. Any contact between the screener and the defensive player inside the three feet was presumed to be an illegal screen or a foul on the offense. The change allowed the screener to close his screen right on the defense as long as the screener wasn't moving. Coach Bob Knight and Coach Bob Boyd were the early practitioners of this offense, which has been very effective for almost three decades. Knight and his Indiana teams enjoyed great success as Knight refined it and expanded its many options. In the seventies, few teams at the college or high school level played an offense that didn't have some relationship to the motion or passing game offense. Time will tell whether the 3-point shot will return the post offense to its former eminence.

Defending the Post Player on the Low Side

Many coaches prefer to have their post player defender playing the low or baseline side. They feel that it is basically the proper position. Fundamentally, they are correct as they have topside help that makes the passing lane narrow if the wing passes the ball outside the shoulder or the opposite side of the post defender. The higher the side defender plays the post player, the more it changes the angle of the pass of the wing player. This changing of the angle increases the threat of a deflection by the frontline help player. Should the offensive post player set an extremely low offensive post, these low-side positions become less effective as the passing lane widens and can eliminate help from a frontline defender.

Movement of the feet is extremely important when siding an offensive post player. Both the high siding and the low siding must depend on quick foot movement if the defender is to lessen the danger of being sealed by the offensive post player.

Defending the Post Player on the High Side

The use of fundamental defensive footwork is probably more important in post defense than in any other phase of individual defense. The position of the ball should dictate the defensive post position. Since the position of the ball changes often, the proper siding of the offensive post player changes. As the defensive siding may change, the use of proper footwork is necessary, as is the decision to roll over the top of the offensive post player or underneath as the change of defensive position occurs.

It is generally accepted that the proper post position defensively when the ball is at the guard positions is the high-inside position if the offensive post player is at a high-side post. A pass from the guard to the post player should not be overplayed in this instance but should be contested to a degree that forces the angle of the pass away from the paint area, however slightly. The danger of an overplay in this instance could cause the offensive post player to effectively employ a seal on the defender. In this instance, a high lob-type pass to the basket area could create an easy basket.

Should the ball move from the strongside guard to the strongside wing player, the defensive post position will change its position. In most instances, the defender will slide underneath on the paint-area side as the offensive post player moves to a medium-post position. Sliding over the top in this instance could allow a lob pass to the basket area that would be difficult to defend. The defensive post position is now on the baseline side as the defender assumes his or her side denial. Some coaches prefer to slide over the top when this position change occurs and feel their backside help will normally defend this lob-type pass.

When the offensive post player comes to the foul-line area, the post defender should assume a ballside position on the shoulder of the offensive post player. An overplay can be vulnerable to a quick cut to the basket by the offensive post player. However, a conservative high-side play will cause the angle of the pass to be less of a threat to an offensive response than an overplay. Some coaches prefer to concede this pass, especially if the offensive post player is not an offensive threat facing the basket. Should this post player be a real threat in the foul-line area, the more aggressive the play of the defender in denying the post pass from the guard.

Summary—Post Defense

There is a tendency to think that adequate post play depends on the ability of the big player to shot block. Too little emphasis is given to the importance of footwork as the movement of position depends on the footwork of the defender. Allowing easy, uncontested passes to a post player, in most instances, is the first step in breaking down the defense. Defending a team that keeps the ball only on the perimeter on offense is much easier than defending a team that not only stretches the defense laterally but also horizontally. The defense should not overcontest in this instance but should not totally concede, either.

The baseline-side defensive player is vulnerable to a seal if the wing passer passes to a teammate at the foul-line area. This situation is particularly true if the low-side or baseline position is too high. The post defender is exposed to a reverse pivot and seal and the entry of a pass from the foul line area to the basket. Should the offensive post player set an extremely low post, a high-side play is preferable, as the passing angle will negate much of an offensive threat.

Playing Behind the Post Player

Playing behind the post player is not a popular post defensive position in most instances. Should the officials allow excessive physical play, a physically strong defender can force a less physical opponent out of the desired position the offensive center wishes to establish. In NBA playoffs, basketball contact is more prevalent and thus allowed. As a result, smaller centers are at a disadvantage. Other levels of basketball, however, usually call the game as consistently in the playoffs as it is called during the regular season.

The danger of playing defense behind a low-posted center is the difficulty of defending without fouling, giving up a very high-percentage hook or lob shot or a step-back type of turnaround shot. The one advantage is the difficulty of sealing a defensive post player. An above-average shot blocker will often concede a low-post position to the opponent, relying on the shot blocking ability the defender possesses. However, the lob shot or banked hook shot is the counter often used to beat the shot blocker.

When a defender physically and aggressively forces the offensive post player from behind, the popular spin move is the effective counter. In this situation, a quick step back will neutralize a spin move in most instances. Basketball is a game of counters, and that is never more apparent than when playing a defensive post. Too often a defensive post player depends too much on size and strength rather than on movement of the feet.

Many successful post defenders will give the opponents different looks. This tactic will create more reading problems for the offense. It is important that the post defender be aware of the weakness of each post defensive position. In teaching post defense, it is important that players know "why" each defensive position is strong and how best to move so the defensive position's weaknesses can't be exploited.

Fronting the Offensive Post Player

A defensive fronting by a large, tall post defensive player creates real problems for the offense. If the hands are held high and backside communication is given, many high-scoring offensive centers are often contained offensively. A front is less effective at a medium-high post and should not be used very often when the offensive center is a side-high post. The defensive problem in these instances is the vulnerability to a seal by the fronted offensive post player on the fronting defender. When an offensive post player is at a medium-high or high-side post position, the defensive player is best situated at a high-side or behind position.

In teaching post defense, it is important that the strengths and weaknesses of each position should be explained and physically demonstrated. As has been often stated, basketball is a game of counters, a game of read and react. Too often we think only of offense when we think of counters and reading, but defensive counters are equally important, especially in post defense.

Defending the Faced-up Post Player

Defending the faced-up post player is the least desirable defensive position for a big defensive post player. Offensive post players with a 15-16 shooting feet range create many problems for slower, less agile defenders. It is important to require post defenders to engage in individual defensive drills that involve playing an offensive player 15-16 feet from the basket. The same mechanics that apply to the wing player defensively should be practiced with the taller post defender. Stance is often the problem as a low, flexed-knee stance is not a normal physical position for the taller player. Basketball being a game of habit simply means that drills that involve a low fundamental stance should be instituted if these taller players are to be functional defensive players in this face-up situation.

A basketball coach should never accept that he or she can't improve foot movement and agility. Tall players are faced with the problem of stance. A comfortable stance is often slow in developing in the tall player. The basic reason is that as these tall players continue to grow, sometimes into their early twenties, their centers of balance consistently change. Because a six-foot player usually stops growth in the teens, his or her center of balance is seldom a problem. A coach, particularly the high school coach, must be patient with tall, growing players since the agility and balance levels of these athletes are slower in developing. Drills instituted for these type of players will expedite the process of improved lateral movement, balance, and the other elements that are typically associated with a growing player.

When faced with a quicker, more agile opponent, the tall player must stay fundamentally within the rules of good defense. If the smaller, quicker player has a 16- to 18-foot shooting range, the defender should try to force this player to a longer range and then back off slightly or to a point that the defender can distract the shooter but still be positioned so that a drive to the basket can be defended. While defensively denying the back cut or high lob pass can be a problem for such a defender, help and communication with good pressure on the ball handler or passer will help to serve as deterrents for the offense in its attacking the taller, less agile defender. Because such a mismatch is a potential weakness for the tall defensive post player, individual drills that address this type of game situation should be regularly employed by coaches in their practice regimen.

Defending the Post Player Off the Ball

Too many defensive centers allow their offensive post opponents to set their position before they begin to assume a defense position. This approach can allow the offensive center a real advantage. Defensive post play can be easier and more effective if the defensive post player initially takes the space or area that the offensive post player desires and which is most productive. Most offensive centers prefer an area from which they best operate. This example can be another indication of the importance of initiative defensively. Making the opposing post player take a position in a less-favorable area helps the defender psychologically.

When the ball is at the wing area or the outside area and the offensive post player is stationed on the opposite side, maintenance of peripheral vision by the defensive post player is absolutely necessary. If vision encompasses only the post player, a high lob pass is a real danger. If the vision encompasses only the ball, it is difficult to detect the offensive post player's movement soon enough to prevent a desirable offensive post position. When playing a post player off the ball, peripheral vision can never be undervalued.

Summary—Defensive Post

Defensive post players should realize that each post defender position has strengths and weaknesses. When these factors are understood, post defensive players can better find ways to strengthen their impact on the post defensive play.

The strength of the baseline, defensive post position on a normal low-post offensive set is that the defensive post player playing the baseline side tries to deny a normal passing angle from a wing position offensive passer. Presumably, the strongside, frontline player sagging to the line of the ball will deter the pass from the wing because of the possibility of interception.

A weakness in defensive rebounding can occur should the baseline defensive play become too high, thereby enabling the offensive post player to gain an inside position should the wing passer decide to shoot. Another problem for the defender is a seal should the wing passer pass to the weakside forward who has flashed to the foul line vicinity. An entry pass into the paint area can allow the opponent an easy basket should the seal on the post player be effective. The defensive counter to this situation is the quick movement over the top or a quick move under. In either case, a slow-reacting defensive post player is vulnerable to an easy basket by the opponent.

Fronting the post also has its problems in the event of an outside shot. Because inside rebounding position is lost when fronting the post player, the fronting defensive player has two principal options—try to regain inside position, if possible, by movement while the ball is in the air, or try to force the inside opponent to a position under the basket where a rebound is less likely to occur on an outside shot. The point to remember is that a fronting position creates a serious problem of controlling the defensive board.

Playing the high side against a medium or a high-side post player can present problems when the ball is at the wing. Should the wing player dribble toward the baseline with one or two short dribbles, the passing angle allows for an easy basket if the offensive post player creates a good seal position and holds it until the wing offensive player actually picks up the ball. If the seal is strong and the pass is accurate and properly angled, it is very difficult to defend as the sealing offensive post player should move his or her seal laterally and keep it until the ball is picked up and the wing player ready to pass. The high-side player also is vulnerable to a seal on an outside shot when attempting to position for the defensive rebound.

The problems of playing behind the post player have been described earlier. A strength of the behind-the-post player position is the defensive screen position whenever the offense shoots the ball. Defensive rebounding can be an important factor in determining the outcome of the game.

STRENGTHS AND WEAKNESSES OF ASSIGNED-INDIVIDUAL DEFENSE

Strengths

A real advantage to the assigned-individual defense is its adaptability. It can, in a sense, dictate to the offense where the defense will allow the shot. It can overplay one side with exaggerated weakside sloughs; it can converge in the basket area if the opponent has a strong inside game but questionable perimeter shooting. It can extend near the midcourt line should it be necessary to upset the opponent's natural spacing and in the course of a game change its position without losing the important physical and mental requirements for a strong team defense. In short, it can stretch from side to side or overplay and extend to better defend one side; furthermore, it can extend horizontally from a tight-basket area defense to an extended forcing defense.

The ability of an assigned-individual defense to exactly pinpoint the individual and team strengths of the opponent's offense allows the defense to know exactly what its responsibilities are. Breakdowns are more easily identified and corrected. Individual mistakes are more noticeable and identifiable. Matching size and ability is a strong positive point of this defense as mismatches are not a problem if the individual defenders realize that they have an individual responsibility to avoid switch situations by aggressive and anticipatory movement. When a player has a defined individual responsibility, few breakdowns occur. The help concept best comes into being in those instances when screens become a real problem for the defender.

One of the features of the individual-assigned defense that gives it real strength is its flexibility. Employing some of the strengths of this defense that relate to zone defense, especially playing off the ball, the lateral switching possibilities of the individual-assigned defense can then negate the effectiveness of lateral offenses. This tactic is another real attribute of this type defense. I am a firm believer not only in team flexibility, but also in individual flexibility by part-method teaching one-on-one, two-on-two, etc. In its various forms, individual ingenuity can be tapped. An example would be an offense that often crosses its guards at the perimeter. The two outside defenders can decide they are going to throw a scare at these offensive frontline people. They alert their backline to a quick, aggressive double on the ball. The backline responds with a three-player high-zoning of any outlet.

Extreme ball pressure—not fouling, but swarming the ball—will sometimes cause the ball handler to panic and throw a blind pass to an imagined, receiving teammate. Sometimes an easy basket results for the defense; sometimes the defense isn't hurt; and sometimes the maneuver will result in an opponent's basket. Regardless, the quick double on the ball will not be forgotten by the opponent, and it will create a less positive attitude about their offense. I call it advertising.

Because this type of defense incorporates a defined individual responsibility on the ball and a defined responsibility off the ball, game preparation can be more concise and much less vague as it applies to defense. If it included only on-the-ball duties, the entire picture of the team's responsibilities would be lessened. The words "focus, commitment" and other one-word descriptions of mental or physical readiness, help defenders to be more aware of their off-the-ball responsibilities. As a result, each individual defender is better able to see the big picture (i.e., the critical need for the team defense) and not just the individual defined aspects of the individual defender. The more the players know and understand about their total responsibilities, the better they will execute their assigned roles.

Basketball has been called a transient game, and it is an apt description. It's not a game like football or baseball that has time intervals between offense and defense, but a game of immediate transition from one phase to the other. Individual responsibility or triangle rebounding is necessary in rebounding in a normally balanced offense. This triangle allows for a court balance in the transition to defense and a communication habit that allows for the defense to reassemble to its normal position with the aid of vocal help. Team defense is very important in this transition situation.

Maybe my strongest positive feeling for this assigned-individual defense is its "we" and "us" concept. Describing this defense, it has invariably been characterized as one player on the ball and four teammates helping. The help concept breeds good team spirit and feeling. It has many positives—a defender diving on the floor for a loose ball recovery will usually result in the defender's teammates treating the ball with care, less apt to shoot a poorly-selected shot, and an appreciation of their teammates' effort in creating a ball possession. Good, solid defensive teams realize the benefits of an opponent's turnover and the point value the defense gives their team when it causes a turnover.

Too often, I believe, coaches underplay the effect, both offensively and defensively, that a turnover creates. The pessimistic coach thinks of the harm it does to the offense and relates the turnover only to what harm it causes the team's offense. The positive, optimistic coach will take a different approach. This coach will sell his or her team on the point value they have gained by the opponent's turnover. An examination of each approach illustrates the value of a positive attitude towards a turnover.

By emphasizing and probably over-emphasizing the team damage a turnover will cause, the negative, while true, can cause undue caution and take away some of a team's offensive aggressiveness and creativity. The old adage, "The person who never made a mistake was the one who never did anything" can apply. Some coaches are more comfortable with the "don't's" than with the "do's." The positive coach is more apt to break down exactly what the point value could reasonably be when they force an opponent's turnover.

A situation that arose in Japan offers an excellent example. The coach of the Isuzu professional team, having been made aware of the detriments of the turnover, really harangued his team on the problem. The more he would yell, the worse the care of the ball became. Necessity being the mother of invention, I suggested a 30-point scrimmage. Japanese players are as competitive as any other players, so the scrimmage would excite their competitive juices. I also suggested a different scoring. Every time a turnover was made, that team had a one-point deduction *and* the opponent not only got the ball but also a point. A slight overkill point-wise, but an issue was involved—value of the ball. As the score reached the 20's, a certain change occurred. During the early part of the scrimmage, one team was ahead 14 to 11. They turned the ball over, and the score became 13 to 12. The ball possession produced a 3-point shot, so now the score was 13 to 15. In short, a 14-12 lead became a 13-to-15 deficit. What occurred was a much better understanding of how a careless pass or inadequate care of the ball can hurt a team. Suddenly, defense becomes more intense, shot selection is better and—most importantly—there is real care of the ball. Granted, the point value can be argued as being too severe, but what is really important is that all the yelling and reproaching by a coach will not validate the importance of a scrimmage conducted along these lines. Why is a turnover such a no-no? Explain it to your players in similar ways and they will get the point.

In 1960, in the West NCAA Regionals, my California Bear team played two games with but one turnover. The opponent in the final regional game hit over 50% on just 44 shots. Cal hit 40% on 68 shots and won by over 20 points. The turnovers were the real answer. Too often the difference in turnovers will reflect the difference in the final score. Because the ball is precious, offensive players should play as though they had bought the ball; on defense, players should act as though the offense had stolen it from them.

Weaknesses

The fact that every defense has its weaker points is another valid reason for the team concept of defense and adopting the strengths of other defenses to complement the individual-assigned defense. Probably the most obvious of the weaker points of an assigned individual defense is its vulnerability to a strong screening attack. Fighting over or under a well-set screen by a sturdy opponent will tax even the best of the assigned defenses. Double screens can create even more of a defensive problem for the individual defender. Dependence on help from the teammate whose player is setting the screen is very important. In the NBA, it is called "show." The teammate off the ball steps up and laterally for a two- or three-second count. The defender being screened must fight over the screen or under the screen to reestablish position on the assigned opponent of the defender.

This situation demands that both defenders understand their responsibilities. There is no switch to consider. The step-up help defender who "shows" will not switch but will contest the ball handler for two to three seconds. The defender being screened must realize that the help teammate momentarily helping must pick up the screener who is a threat cutting to the basket after the screen.

A coach must be explicit in what he or she wants in this situation. Both roles must be defined precisely as to each player's responsibilities. If a coach is vague, numerous problems can arise. Being slow getting by the screen and to the ball handler who has used the screen to set up a drive or a shot could result in an unopposed open shot.

A lack of communication will cause the two defenders to pick up the ball and leave the screener open for an easy basket, or, if both defenders pick up the screener who has cut to the basket, an open shot will be created for the ball handler. Properly playing a screen on the ball requires teaching and explaining each defined role in a clear but demanding voice by the coach. This situation is a real test for an assigned-individual defense, and there should be no gray areas.

An aggressive, contesting defense will often commit fouls. It is difficult to be aggressive in denying the ball, fighting over screens, physically playing a post player and an adept, quick drive by an individual and not foul. Zone defenses and the switch defense have far fewer problems with defensive fouling.

The overcommitment of some defenders to holding their assigned opponent down in points will often cause these defenders to be lax in their off-the-ball responsibilities. Weakside help can suffer, and a breakdown in communication can occur as the defender gets too absorbed with the assignment of holding down the assigned opponent and forgets the importance of not letting teammates down by their communication breakdowns.

The assigned-individual defense does not complement a fast-break attack as does a zone and even some switch-defense teams. A zone has its personnel best positioned for the conversion from defense to offense because a zone's ball handlers are out front and the taller players are in the basket area. The same alignment prevails for some switch defenses. An assigned individual defense has, for example, each of its players, when converting to offense from defense, in many different places on the court. The ball-handling guard may be covering his or her opponent in the corner and not be positioned for a quick fast break. This same defender could be under the basket defending a post player. The variance of where the defenders are positioned when the shot is taken can create a problem in conversion, since the ball handlers are often poorly positioned for the quick outlet.

To play this defense properly, the defenders must be in movement every time the ball moves, either by a pass or a dribble. This movement requires superb conditioning. A zone defense and the switch defense are much less demanding. In the individual-assigned defense, the defender is charged with denying the assigned opponent the ball in most instances, playing the offensive player from sideline to sideline, quickly picking up the opponent in transition, defending a dribbler in isolation situations, and, in general, being continually ready for movement. These responsibilities require excellent conditioning since one defender not properly conditioned can break down the entire team defense. There are no short cuts to a defense that is consistent in its five-player defensive movement.

The ability of this defense to adapt lessens the effect its weaker aspects create. Again, the flexibility that allows for adjustment reduces the impact that these weaker elements can cause.

CHAPTER 4

SITUATIONAL DEFENSES

The Double-Down Defense

The double-down defense is probably the most publicized defense in the NBA today. It is being employed by more college and high school coaches as the post-type offense has become more popular. Doubling a talented post player goes back to George Mikan in the middle to late 1940's and early 1950's. Its purposes were different from the strategy for its use in the NBA today. It is entirely possible that it will be an effective tactic in the future as the coaches realize how effective it can be in certain situations. A number of sound reasons exist for employing the double-down defense, including:

- to reduce the effectiveness of a high-scoring, talented offensive post player
- to induce the post player to pass out of the double-down to a lesser offensive threat
- to be part of a planned defensive tactic in delaying the pass from the wing or guard into the low-posting center until there are but eight or less seconds left on the time clock. Because of limited shot options, the time-clock pressure will cause the post player to pass out to the perimeter
- to create recognition problems for the post player by varying the double-down player from a weakside, frontline defender to a weakside, backline defender or one of the strongside defenders

While the double-down in the NBA is effective in many situations, its use would be of a different nature for the high school and college coach. The double-down is the direct cause of the low-scoring problem today in the NBA as the coaches have learned to use the 24-second clock to their defensive advantage. Simply, the strategy is for the defense to delay the advance of the ball to the forecourt for approximately eight seconds, force the ball pick-up at the sideline, and deny—but not overdeny—the wing or center outlet, thereby creating a time problem for the offense to start its half-court offense from their normal spacing. The defense will then allow a wing release and a post pass to a low-post center. It's at this point that the double-down commences. The defensive post player will slide to a baseline side position, and the double-down will attempt to discourage the post player from a path to the middle. It is extremely important that the double-down defender is most concerned with taking away the step to the paint area of the post player. Because this path must be taken away, it's essential that the step of the post player is shut off. The overplay of the post defender toward the baseline will take away post movement in that direction. Turnaround shots are a shooting option, but not much else is open unless the post player decides to power the shot over the defender and risk an offensive foul. What usually occurs is the pass to the perimeter, leaving few seconds on the clock.

The 30- or 35-second clock will negate this type of defensive scheme. However, it could be a situational-type defense used for the same reasons as the run-and-jump or other doubling defensive employments. With 10 seconds left on the clock, it could be effectively used at the high school or college levels of play. When the double-down does occur, the three perimeter defenders employ a zone-type outside defense.

It has been my experience and conviction that these types of defensive maneuvers don't compromise the defensive integrity if you are committed to the individually-assigned type of defense. As with the zone press, the run-and-jump and other similar situational defenses, such as switch, zone or the individual-assigned defense principles may be employed, but each defense is a defense in itself. Compromising the principles of the assigned-individual defense occurs when the half-court defense is changed and different principles of vision, position, responsibility, and, particularly, the mental requirements are changed. These types of situational defenses are complete in their basics as to what they demand for them to be successful. With the exception of the double-down defense on the post-up player, none would be considered a normally-spaced, half-court defense.

Defending Screen on the Ball

Defending a screen on the ball is one of the most difficult defensive situations to effectively control in the NBA. In college and high school competitions, it isn't such a problem. Regardless, it can be effective at any level of defensive basketball play. Again, rules are a major factor in its success. In the NBA, the no-zone rule interpretation can take away the weakside support to a large degree if the off-the-ball offensive players are spaced on the weakside. The other areas of competition that do not have a no-zone rule can give much better weakside help to the defenders who have to cope with the screen on the play. It's interesting to note that FIBA (the Federation International Basketball Association, which governs all segments of world basketball play but the USA) does not abide by the no-zone rule, nor do our different levels of American amateur basketball competition.

A coach should always precisely define individual responsibilities to his or her team. Probably in this screen-on-the-ball deployment, it is more important than in any other single phase. Indecision, slow reactions, and poor teamwork often result because of a communication or defined-responsibility problem.

The center screen on the defender of the wing man is usually an effective screen by a big body on a smaller body. The defender playing the wing man and being screened must be made to realize there is no switch option. Simply stated, this defender has two options. The first option is to fight over the top of the screen and get to the wing man with the ball who has dribbled over the screener, leaving little room for the defender. Nevertheless, the ball defender pursues the wing man with the ball. The second option is to go under the screen. Taking this route can result in an open outside shot if the wing man stops the dribble suddenly and spots up for an open shot. Sliding underneath will cause the defender a real problem getting back to the ball handler.

In the case of the first option, the defensive center must step up and lend support to his or her teammate who is trying to get to the wing teammate by fighting over the top of the screen. This defensive center does what is called "show." However, the "show" is for only two or three counts. This defender then picks up the center screener. The defender must realize that the teammate helping will help but for these few seconds. No excuses can be accepted if the wing defender doesn't aggressively fight over this screen and pick up the ball handler or wing player. Each responsibility is clearly defined.

Switch Defense

The great popularity of the switch defense came during the pre-World War II days in the 1930s. Its strengths were that it complemented a fast break, reduced defensive fouls, and was able to avoid mismatches—as its theory of personnel was to have players of generally equal size. This factor gave it an advantage because players of equal size precluded offensive mismatches, especially in rebounding. The Stanford University team that won the 1941 NCAA Championship was the model of the personnel requirements coaches at that time were seeking. A picture of this team shows little height or size difference between all five players. The Stanford team's success was testimony to the coaches who had adapted the switch defense theory.

Prior to the elimination of the center jump in the late '30s, the fast-break advantage was not a reason initially advanced for the use of the switch defnse. The other virtues of the switch defense, however, impressed many coaches. A strength the zone defense has always presented to its adherents is the placement of its personnel. The quicker ball handlers were frontline defenders who switched on all lateral and vertical crosses. This switching ensured that the defenders were in the proper place when transition from defense to offense occurred. It was considered a complementary defense for the offense. After the elimination of the center jump, the switch defense became really popular for this fast-break transition concept.

The mismatch concept was a real problem for teams that didn't incorporate midpoint vision in their weakside defensive play. Because the East and many areas of the Midwest played this type of off-the-ball defense, backside post help was not practiced to any extent. The switch defense enabled the back defenders to defend opponents in the basket area. The Stanford team was coached by one of the great basketball coaches and a leading figure in guiding the college game of basketball in these earlier times—Everett Dean. A former Indiana University mentor who was considered one of the top coaches and innovators in basketball, he brought this switch concept to the West. Because teams in the West were schooled in weakside vision and help by the weakside defenders, Dean's tactic was not accepted as readily as in the East and Middle West.

Another strength identified with the switch defense was its strength against a screen. A weakness of an individually-assigned defense is its vulnerability to a strong screening offense. The switch reduced this problem drastically. What was also considered a positive feature of the switch dense was that less energy was exhausted as opposed to what the individual player expended on player defense. This attribute has always been a positive factor for featuring zone offense, and it's difficult to refute this feature.

The lessening of the probability of fouls, the conservation of energy, and the complementary features that this defense gives to the fast break are the primary reasons for adopting the switch defense. There are others of lesser magnitude but none of the importance of these three.

There are, however, disadvantages that can be attributed to the switch defense. An offense tries to create a shot opportunity by causing a defender to be caught up in a good, effective screen. In theory, you attack the individual defense by congestion (screener or screeners), but a switch must be attacked in the middle, i.e, simply running an offensive player between the two switch defenders. This theory is particularly effective when a screen on the ball movement occurs. Usually, it's a center screening on a forward or a wing defender. A mismatch can easily occur on a switch as the defensive center must pick up the forward, while the screening center will reverse pivot seal and make a vee cut to the basket with the smaller forward then having to defend the bigger center. This example is but one instance of attacking a switch. A play that is even more difficult for two switching teammates is when the offensive man fakes a screen and proceeds directly to the basket between the two defenders. Often neither players picks up this slicing offensive player or goes to pick up the slicer, and no one defends the player with the ball. We call this a "slip screen."

Another negative of the switch defense is the tendency of a switch team to become soft. This is a real possibility. The major concern of individual responsibility is more toward position than individual responsibility. However, I believe switching laterally between defenders can give the defense more positives than negatives. Good, strong, backline single and double screens can be difficult to defend without help. In the front line, the defensive guards can work closely together and defend against the ball handler's penetration, forcing the outside perimeter line of defense inside the foul line. Some predictable teams can be vulnerable to a quick double of the ball by the two defensive guards, while a quick three-player high zone by the back defenders can create problems for the offense. Also, a residual of this type of tactic can induce a defensive mindset by the two opposing offensive guards.

It is important that proper mechanics be employed when switching. The switch should always be called by the back defender—and in a lateral situation. It is very important for the coach to stress the responsibilities of each defender. Backscreens, in particular, must be called loud and clear or a team will be exposed to an easy basket with two players on the ball and no one playing the screener who has sliced to the basket.

Another fundamental of the switch is that the player who has been away from the ball but now switches to pick up the ball handler should always switch up. The purpose, basically, is to have pressure on the ball. A lateral switch without ball pressure gives the ball handler several options. A lateral switch is like the "prevent" defense in football; the ball handler can review the options he or she may have.

As has been previously stated, coaches should try to assimilate into their defensive schemes the strengths of each defense that they feel will not lessen the integrity and consistency of their team's defensive play. Also, the wise coach learns all he or she can about each defense so that their offense will know how best to attack it. Because the switch defense has not been widely accepted in the past three or four decades, most coaches have a limited degree of familiarity with it and thus have problems attacking it.

The Change-up Defense

This type of defense is currently extremely popular. However, it has been an integral part of defensive schemes since the '30s. Its first employment was the change of one type of zone to another type. Today, its strength rests in its change from various types of assigned-individual defenses to the wide variety of traps currently used by the college and high school coaches in the game. Because basketball is simply a game of counters, the reading and responding by the offense is more difficult because of the many different defenses with which the offense must contend.

As proposed earlier, the proponents prefer this change-up defense because of the difficulty the offense has in reading and adjusting. The opponents of this type of defense believe it is less effective in the latter stages of the season. Their reasoning is that the more experience a team has facing a certain type defense, the easier it becomes for the offense to adjust and favorably attack it. Other rationales of the proponents and opponents of the change-up defense exist. Collectively, these are the situations a basketball coach is faced with, and they are examples of why basketball coaching is so challenging.

The basketball coach has many considerations, some of which are often contradictory, when planning his or her style of play. The various levels of play—elementary, high school, college, professional and even foreign play—each present problems that are a part of their level of competition but different from the other levels of basketball competition.

As basketball coaches, we are conditioned in our knowledge and approach by our experiences as players, by what we have read, heard or seen, by the influences a successful coach and his or her program may exert, and most certainly by the various coaches who were our mentors and those we may have served as assistants when preparing for head coaching opportunities. Regardless of the extent of these influences in shaping the philosophy and play of the head coach, it is absolutely necessary that the coach make decisions with which he or she is comfortable. We all borrow, use and refine ideas of others, but they must be in conformity to that with which we can comfortably live.

The change-up defense offers an example of what I have proposed. Practice-time allotments, physical and mental limitations for whatever reasons and attitudes that don't lend themselves to an aggressive denial-type defense, a lack of foot speed that precludes much use or a desire for a press-type defense are reasons for considering the change-up type defense. A mentally alert team that can understand its strengths and weaknesses will often benefit by this type defense.

It is basic that the offense must correctly read the defense before it can expect to successfully attack it. It is also basic, at least in most coaches' minds, that a zone defense creates a different problem for the offense than does an assigned-individual defense or even a switch defense. To further complicate the reading problem of the offense, what works best against a 1-3-1 defense does not normally work well against a 2-1-2 or a 2-3 zone. Some of the longest nights coaches may ever have is when their offense has a reading problem against this change-up defense.

The change-up defense can be a problem at any period of an opponent's schedule. Under most circumstances, it is more effective in the early part of the year. At that time, most teams are usually struggling, trying to establish an offensive rhythm; they are less quick to pick up the defensive change, recognize exactly what the change is and properly space themselves to attack the defense. As the season develops, the adjustment to change often comes quicker as teams have learned from earlier mistakes. Because the better teams seem to adjust quicker, this defense has never been a real factor in college championships or high school championships. However, it is more widely employed today than ever before. Basketball, being a game of counters, as has been so often stated, it may take that step in the future that permits the change-up defense to be more readily accepted by coaches at all levels. Maybe it's a case of never saying "never."

As rules and re-interpretation of rules are introduced to the game, a coach must examine the change in the game that so often accompanies these changes. Should the ball possession rule be lowered to 30 seconds, the change-up defense takes on much more importance. A case in point is the 24-second clock and the NBA. By use of the double-down defense that accompanies the full-court, ball harassing-type defense with a denial of the pass up court, post offenses have been greatly reduced in their effectiveness. The time problem of the 24-second clock has caused the game to slow down to a walk, with the 3-point shot the result as the offense tries to beat the 24-second clock. This situation is a clear case of coaches making a rule—the 24-second clock—work to the defense's advantage. The change-up defense can be effective if the offense has not established its shot and has but eight or less seconds left on the shot clock. A change to an aggressive run-and-jump, side-court trap with a denial of immediate outlets can cause a panic reaction by the offense. The threat of not beating the possession time clock is a psychological advantage for the defense as the offense often hurries bad shots, forces passes and loses its composure in these change-up instances.

The change-up defense can create more effectiveness if it encompasses a change of defensive tempo as well as a change of type of defense. Most coaches would agree that a soft-type, half-court defense will normally be less effective against a lateral, downscreening type of offense. Conversely, the same type offense will be less effective against a more aggressive, denial-type defense. As a result, when a change-up defense changes the tempo of its defense, it creates even more problems for the offense. This more aggressive defense negates to a great extent a lateral-type offensive reaction but is less effective against back-door diagonal or straight-line cuts to the basket. For the offense to immediately react to the proper counters is not a simple task for the offense, and until they do, the defense has a real advantage.

Strengths of the Change-up Defense:

- Reading problem for opponent
- Particularly effective against inexperienced guards
- Impatience in opponents
- Confusion it can create for a superior talented opponent
- Preparation problems for an opponent
- Defensive confidence it can inspire when the opponent becomes confused
- Forcing opponent to have to -counter each change of defense
- Forcing opponent to resort to low-percentage shots when unable to fathom the changes.
- Turnovers it can create which often result in easy, unopposed baskets
- Changing the tempo of the defense
- Defensively using the ball-possession clock to its advantage

Weaknesses of the Change-up Defense:

- It is usually more effective in the early part of the schedule than in the important late-season games and post-season tourneys.
- It can create problems of vision, stance, responsibility as it changes from the assigned individual defense to a zone-type defense, or vice versa.
- As opponents experience more defenses of this type, their reading and counters become more effective.
- Being able to go from a soft-type defense to an aggressive denial-type defense as a unit can be difficult.
- This surprise-and-change concept has not produced many final four NCAA teams nor high school championship teams as opposed to the simplicity and execution programs.
- Breakdowns can occur for a solid, aggressive denial team that relies on peripheral vision and low stance and is mentally prepared for its individual-assigned responsibilities.
- The fundamental habits that are essential to a particular aspect of the change-up defense can be compromised, thereby lessening the effectiveness of this specific phase of the change-up defense.

Summary—Change-up Defense

There are many factors that should determine the basic defense a coach decides to play. The strengths of each defense—and the weaknesses—should be studied before hard decisions concerning what defense to play are made. Coaches should acknowledge that every defense has weaknesses that are inherent in it regardless of a team's personnel strengths. Sometimes above-average personnel or an experienced team can minimize these inherent weaknesses. Quickness—physically and mentally—is extremely necessary in effective team defensive play. For a coach to simply dismiss a defense without analyzing its potentiality for that coach's team, or parts of it that could become a part of his or her team's defensive schemes, is not wise.

The change-up type defense, despite its weaknesses, could be the proper defense for some teams regardless of its limitations. By studying and responding to its strengths and weaknesses, coaches who have teams that have limited talent and limiting attributes that would otherwise make the assigned-designated defense difficult to effectively employ could resort to the surprise-and-change theory. By changing the type of defense and the tempo of the defensive changes, a less-talented team could be able to stay competitive and sometimes upset more talented opponents. Rather than burden a team initially with many change-up defenses, it would be nice to build the change-up concept more slowly and add to it as the season progresses. It is better to do a few things well than many things only fairly well. Coaches should study the strengths and weaknesses of the change-up defense, use those strengths that best serve their personnel and understand its weaknesses in order to minimize their effect on their team.

CHAPTER 5

ZONE DEFENSES

The number or type of strictly zone defenses has not changed to any extent in the past three or four decades. The interchange of zone types during the course of the game is more popular with today's coaches as the change from one type to a different formation or type creates different passing lanes and shooting areas. The importance of the offense quickly reading the change is of much importance, especially with a time possession clock being a factor the offense must always consider.

While the types are similar, the methods of attacking a zone have really changed over the span of time. Traditionally, the use of the dribble was a no-no. 'Don't cross-court pass' was another rule. Initially, many zone coaches perfected one type and stayed with it. Clair Bee was the first highly visible coach to play the 1-3-1 and has been credited with its introduction into the game. If you played Clair Bee's Long Island team, you were facing a 1-3-1 zone with no frills, maybe slight adjustments if needed, but a 1-3-1 nevertheless. Penn State was a conventional 2-1-2 type that never changed but would slightly adjust as needed. Because the zone coach played the same zone, the ability of the players to perform their responsibilities was made easier. They were extremely difficult zones to attack. They weren't expected to assume different responsibilities as a 1-3-1 zone became a 2-3 or another zone with a different alignment and different responsibilities. There were few gray areas when the zone alignment was consistent.

The first teams and coach that I saw attack the crease were the Indiana teams of Coach Bobby Knight in the '70s. The simplicity of forcing two perimeter defenders to defend the gap and the ball immediately gave the offense a real advantage of numbers—four offensive well-spaced players against three zone defenders. Quick movement of the ball usually caused the defense to give up an open perimeter shot or an open player inside. While not as effective today as it was in the '70s and '80s, it still presents real problems to the zone.

Another factor that has caused changes is the shot clock. Without any particular need to hurry their zone offenses, coaches would stress patience when attacking a set zone. Probably, the clock has caused many coaches to change their team's zone alignment during the course of an opponent's ball possession to confuse the offense. It will cause a hurried pass, a poor shot selection and a loss of composure for the offense if this change of zone occurs in the last 10 seconds of ball possession.

Another very important change was the institution of the three-point shot line. If nothing else, for many coaches it revised the old adage that if one is to be beaten, it will not be inside but over the top. This rule brought in more frequent uses of the 3-2 zone alignment. Presumably, the three-point line can best be defended by a 3-2. While it is more vulnerable inside, the point value of the three-point shot seemed to prevail among many coaches that the outside area is the first defensive option. A coach must also factor in the strengths of the opponent. If the opponent is very strong inside but has a weak perimeter-shooting problem, then this type defense would be a problem. If the reverse is true, then it can be effective, especially if a team is ahead and the opponent must rely on the three-point shot to get back into the game.

Detailing some of the basic fundamentals of a zone defense are involves relating these fundamentals as to how they differ from the assigned-individual defense. Knowing these differences can help a coach better understand the basics of a zone defense, including the following:

- *Position:* In the zone concept, this fundamental relates to the position of the ball as to the individual responsibilities of the zone defender. In the assigned-individual defense, position relates to the opponent.

- *Vision:* In the zone defense, vision is on the ball and the area assigned to the individuals. In the assigned-individual concept, the vision is at the midpoint to see the ball and the assigned opponent.

- *Responsibilities:* In the zone, the area of coverage is specifically detailed to each zone member regardless of the alignment. If the defender overextends and goes beyond the perimeter of the zone area, the zone defender can cause a real breakdown of the total. In the assigned-individual defense, the responsibilities are clearly defined as to the strengths and limitations of the opponent. If the opponent is an outside threat with little threat to drive to basket, the defender can deny the entry and play tight on the ball if the opponent is within the range of his or her effective shot. Again, the reverse if the opponent is a good driver but poor shooter. From a coaching standpoint, defensive breakdowns are much easier to see and understand what corrections are needed in an individual-assigned defense. In a zone, it is often difficult to immediately identify the particular strengths of the opponent as he or she is not identified until they are in the particular zone area.

- *Stance:* A zone usually calls for hands up and away with a high and sometimes a bouncy stance. Often, the legs are stiff. The assigned-individual defender is taught to be in a low-based, flexed-knee stance with arms up and away from the body. This defender must stay low with good vision because of the possibility of a back screen, a side screen, or a speed cut from the weakside to the strongside area of the offense.

Several basic reasons exist for employing a zone defense, including:

Personnel

Young, inexperienced players will more quickly adapt to a zone defense. The assigned-individual defense commands many different responsibilities. It's a defense that will improve and get more effective and resilient as the players gain experience. The zone can be taught more quickly and be effective earlier than with a young team trying to play the individual defense.

Slower but bigger players who would be physically too slow to be effective in an assigned-individual defense can be effective inside. As such, the type of zone employed can take these strengths and limitations into account when determining the type of zone alignment.

A particularly strong rebounder and shot blocker can be best used in a zone that will ensure the defensive presence of this player in the paint area. Conversely, an assigned-individual defense can cause this same player to be defending the opponent 16-18 feet from the basket.

Smaller but quicker people can be a defensive liability if they are playing an individual-assigned defense. For example, their opponents take them inside and post them up. A zone defense can prevent this situation from happening, although the particular zone and the zone responsibility assigned may be affected by the physical attributes of the defenders. For example, the NBA, adhering to its antiquated no-zone rule, eliminates many outstanding small players who can help teams in so many ways. Few NBA teams will take a chance on the small player because of the no-zone rule. Personally, I don't agree, as I weigh this post-up problem against the many assets smaller players bring to the game—quickness, improved transition, passing and penetration skills and fan appeal. Additionally, they can give added strength to the overall defense because of their quickness and skillsat playing the press or individual defense in the back and midcourt. It's not exactly the case of one being worried about the mosquitoes while being trampled by the elephants, but it's close.

Organizational Problems

Organizational problems vary to a great extent because of the conditions various programs face. Many high school coaches are faced with limited time, less than normal-sized courts, players joining the basketball program after the football-playing season has ended, sharing the court facilities with other sports, having a specified amount of time for the court use, and dividing up three different basketball teams. These are examples of some of the problems the high school coach and small college coach must face. as such, because of space and time limitations, the zone defense is a more practical defense because the coach will have more time to work on his or her team's offensive game. Sometimes what we would like to do is just a practical answer to the many problems of this nature the coach faces. If a court is at minimal-lateral length, the zone can be more effective. A shorter court will help a slower team.

Fouls

Another advantage a zone defense can create is a minimal number of fouls. Avoiding foul problems can help a team keep its star player from being handicapped by early fouls, keep its opponent off the foul line much longer, and, because of the relative paucity of fouls, allow it to play with assurance and confidence. Individuals and teams with excessive fouls will normally lose their aggressiveness, alertness and spontaneity, determination and other important facets of a strong defense. Many important games are decided on this one factor—excessive fouls. In the latter stages of a game, a coach wants his or her best players playing their normal defensive game, not intimidated by the foul situation, and free of any restraint a foul may cause.

A zone defense can reduce the normal effectiveness of a team that relies on two-man action, a screen attack, one-on-one isolation ability, or an unprincipled freelance style of play. While these particular movements are problems for an assigned-individual defense, they are not a significant problem for a zone defense. Dribbling is held to a minimum, and other than attacking a crease in a zone, is not of real importance in attacking a zone. Many teams have a problem adjusting their tempo going from a movement, slashing-type of offense against an individual defense to a slower tempo as their team adjusts to the zone. Often, these teams face an additional problem—resuming the tempo and timing they had if they go from one offense to a zone offense and back to their original offense. Sometimes, a team that is having difficulty with its individual defense will change to a zone for only a few possessions and then go back to their original defense, which can become more effective since the offense often cannot find the same rhythm of movement they originally displayed. Interrupting the flow of an opponent that has been difficult to stem can be changed by several different defensive maneuvers—and this tactic is one of them.

Little doubt exists that a zone defense best complements a fast-break offense. The zone will normally ensure that the outside defender and best ball handler will be positioned to initiate the fast break. The bigger inside player will likewise be positioned to gather the rebound and pass the ball out to the normal outlets. An assigned-individual defense may have the best ball handler defending a post-up player and the rebounding outlet player playing an opponent at the wing 20 feet from the basket and the rebound. As such, a zone defense is a strong complement to a fast break offense.

Summary—Zone Defenses

Surprise and change are valid reasons for the use of the zone defense. As pointed out previously in this book, habits properly inculcated are the real strength of an assigned-individual defense. The basic tenets that are associated with an individual-assigned defense—stance, vision, position and the aggressive mental aspects—are compromised when the defense shifts to a zone. As stated earlier, the stance, vision and position employed in the two types of defenses are basically different. The nature of a zone defense is that it is a passive defense. By compromising the physical habits and tenets of the assigned-individual defense, a weakening and reduced-aggressive mental outlook occurs when both of these defenses are employed in a game. The school of teaching as it applies to an assigned-individual defense is one of simplicity and execution. It's hard to argue that most team champions at all levels of competition are usually from the simplicity and execution school. A defense that is predictable, but capable of adjusting within its rules of coping with the opponents' game plan, offers the best opportunity for success.

However, as I have stated, the many reasons for the use of a zone defense may outweigh the importance of the simplicity and execution theory. In that regard, some coaches and programs try to gain several of the advantages that the defensive change to a zone can give but make their zone as simple as possible. For example, Coach Mike Krzyzewski at Duke purposely does not practice a zone defense to any extent and merely uses the change to create adjustment problems for his opponent. He feels he can keep the defensive intensity of his assigned-individual defense with this approach. I'm not sure he isn't right.

Valid, defensible reasons exist for using a zone defense. If these reasons outweigh the negative factors, it would be wise to consider the zone. A coach should keep in mind that personnel, facilities, time, and other factors considered can be sufficient reasons for employing a zone. It's an individual coaching decision that can be best implemented if the coach thoughtfully and clearly examines the various elements involved.

Box-and-One

In some instances, the primary reason for deploying a box-and-one is to create an adjustment problem for the opponent. In other situations, it's use is dictated by the coach's decision that the star player of the opposing team is too difficult to defend by a single defender without help. Because the four teammates of the single defender are positioned in their box-type spacing, the single defender can overplay and concentrate on ball denial to this star offensive opponent. The box-type spacing assures the single defender of back help.

The box-and-one has been the most popular type of zone defense for many years. It was the first defense of this type I ever encountered in coaching, and it demands preparation by the offense to effectively attack it.

Diamond-and-One

Similar to the box-and-one, the primary purpose of a diamond-and-one is to help a defender guard a high-scoring opponent. Some offenses counter by placing the scoring opponent into the middle or foul line and make it a 1-3-1. Although the diamond-and-one is as popular as the box-and-one, if it is not attacked properly, it can be very effective.

Other types of these defenses are seen each year. The two previously described are the most common. In the 1998 NCAR Regional Final in the West, a defense not commonly used was employed by Utah against the defending 1998 NCAA champion, Arizona. Some media called it a 2-3 with the frontline defenders playing straight man defense and the back three in a lateral zone. It was an effective strategy by Utah, since it is relatively difficult to adjust to the unexpected in the NCAA tournament. Actually, Utah's back three defenders effectively switched on all of the lateral movement of the offense. I saw Utah play three games in the NCAA tourney, but I never was aware of this defensive maneuver. The manner in which Utah played their defense showed they had a familiarity with the defense, as it was beautifully executed. I doubt in such an important game that a defense with which the defense has no experience could be so well played.

Sometimes a team's personnel is such that a coach must be creative. It's a good approach if a coach has a team capable of going far in the post-season tournaments. It can be a part of a coach's pre-season planning to include defensive maneuvers that could be useful in the important late season play. Games that a coach feels will not be as much of a problem as others, and relatively unimportant league games, are situations that could be used to experiment with these types of defenses. Also, such an approach can heighten the level of practice interest of the players as the defense is described to them. Another advantage is for the coach to be able to better refine the mechanics if he or she has the opportunity to study the defense. I always found that incorporating situations like this in practices can occasionally add a sense of spice and curiosity. Practices can become dull, especially in the latter stages of the season, and these types of additions are usually welcomed by the team.

Summary—Situational Zone Defenses

Situational defenses have many purposes. They can give a team another important dimension for an opponent to have to prepare for. Most fundamentally-sound defensive teams have a large degree of predictability. However, most coaches who believe in the predictability concept, and follow it, still leave room for creativity. As long as fundamental principles are not compromised, I am a firm believer in creativity. It can add spice to the coach's thinking.

Match-up Zone

When the history of the various aspects of basketball is studied, it is always interesting to learn that concepts and types of plays that seem new are merely refinements of what was employed in the past.

What comes to mind is motion offense. Coach Henry Iba, the former coach of the Oklahoma Aggies, used a similar motion. Because of the screen rule at the time, it was not as effective as the offensive set is today. It was termed the passing game. The change of the screen rule from a three-foot area, legal-screen distance to a position where the screener is permitted directly on the opponent who is being screened changed the effectiveness of the screen. Bobby Knight, with the help of Bob Boyd, the well-respected coach of the University of Southern California Trojans, refined this offense that soon became the most popular offense in the history of the game. Called motion offense, this offense has been the most popular offense in high school and college basketball. Coach Iba originally was introduced to this offensive concept by a high school coach in Oklahoma. He refined it and made it a very successful part of his great career. Coach Knight took it another step to its present dominance in high school and college basketball play. Defenses and various other parts of the game have had similar histories.

Another example of a basketball element that has had a significant history of change and importance in this game is the stall pattern. In the '30s, I was introduced to an offense that I had never seen. It deployed players in the four corners of the offensive end of the court with the ball handler outside the top of the circle in midcourt as it relates to the sidelines. Actually, it wasn't much of an offense. As a defender, however, I found myself chasing my opponent all over the offensive court continuously without a lot of success. When I began coaching, my experience as a player induced me to try it out as a stall. It was an integral part of our winning the 1949 NIT. I called it the "3-out-and-two-in" stall. A number of years later, Dean Smith refined it and called it the "four-corner" offense. Subsequently, it became a very popular stall offense. The recent rule changes—the 35-second clock and the 5-second count on the ball handler by a defender positioned within a defensive position—has reduced its use today. This example is cited to make coaches realize that very few individuals have really invented new theories. In fact, what these individuals did was to refine what elements impressed them. Someone once said the only one who has really invented anything in basketball was its inventor, John Naismith. Most defenses, other than the press types of defense, have origins that date back to the early days of the game.

The match-up zone defense gained great popularity in the '70s and '80s. Coach Boyd Grant has been properly given credit for its effectiveness and its adoption by many coaches as their standard defense. This defense was a principal reason for Coach Grant's Fresno State team upsetting its opponents in the NIT. Emerging as the NIT champion, Fresno State's success gave credence to this type of defense. The one common denominator of any phase that gains national popularity is its being given a name. The match-up zone is such an instance.

Well before the advent of Boyd Grant's match-up zone, a similar type of defense many of us called the Philly defense was causing offenses real problems. The creator of this defense was Coach Harry Litwack of Temple University. Frankly, it was the most difficult defense to attack that I ever encountered. Like the match-up, it was a part-zone, part-man defense. Using it, Temple was able to progress to the Final Four in the late '50s. Various forms of Coach Litwack's defense subsequently became more common. When Coach Grant's team won the NIT, he gave it a name as he refined Coach Litwack's concepts. The match-up is still a successful and popular defense.

RULES OF THE MATCH-UP ZONE

- Pressure the ball at all times
- Jump to pass with all five players—keep zone tight
- Remember that the second man always rolls to penetration
- Play with hands up
- Never get beat in paint
- Have all five players rebound
- Pin the ball on sideline and fight dribble reverse
- Be aware that closeouts are important
- At no time do you guard air—always guard someone!

RESPONSIBILITIES IN THE MATCH-UP ZONE

Guards
- Pressure the ball and push the sideline
- Protect the ballside elbow—do not allow in-post flashes
- Sprint in your recovery
- Trap penetration
- Recognize 2-versus-1 on sideline
- Be a rebounder

Forwards and Centers
- Stop the post pass
- Collapse to the ball in the paint
- Play with your hands up
- Sprint in your recovery
- Rebound all shots
- Recognize 2-versus-1 (bump off on baseline cut or help guards get back home)
- Pressure the ball
- Trap penetration

CHAPTER 6

REBOUNDING

Many different theories have been advanced relating to effective offensive and defensive rebounding. Ball possession is such an important facet of the game, it is only logical for a coach to study the various methods and approaches and teach what best serves the fundamental concepts of the game. Different approaches exist when teaching offensive rebounding and defensive rebounding. Offense rebounding encompasses more of the mental aspects of the game—e.g., resourcefulness, aggressiveness, discipline, movements to entice the defensive rebounder to react away from the area the offensive rebounder wishes to counter, etc. The term "garbage man" is frequently used to describe an effective and often under-sized offensive rebounder. Conversely, the defensive rebounder must rely more on technique and less on athleticism and opportunism. That dictum may help explain coaches' beliefs as they apply to rebounding. Yet, some coaches don't believe in the defensive screening theory, while others may demand a premature action of movement by the offensive rebounder.

Similar to many aspects of the game of basketball, coaches have varied approaches to rebounding. Whatever a coach decides, however, a need exists for consistency of approach. The primary responsibility of a defensive rebounder is simply to keep the defensive rebounder's body between the ball and the offensive rebounding opponent. If possible, the defensive screen should be executed six or more feet from the basket. A fundamental precept of ball recovery is that the defensive rebounder should be at approximately a 40-degree angle as the recovery of the ball occurs. Again, why? The angle keeps the recovery protected as the descent begins. Only by fouling the defensive rebounder can the offensive rebounder touch the ball. Without the proper body angle, the defender often has the ball legally stripped as the opposing rebounder descends.

The mechanics vary slightly with each defensive rebounder as they apply to position and responsibility. Playing and screening a shooter will differ from that of the weakside, backline defender, who also must give help defense to the defensive post players. Obviously, the distances vary to a great degree between the player on the shooter and the player giving help. The center or post player has a different problem from the other two. The responsibilities and mechanics as they apply to the various positions are discussed in the following sections.

On-the-Ball or the Shooter

Because the defender is positioned closely to the shooter, the defensive rebounder can often make immediate contact. Usually, the shooter is in a face-up position, so it's important to immediately screen and make contact. By making immediate contact, the defender reduces the effectiveness of the offensive rebounder by not allowing the offensive rebounder to gather speed, quickness and agility. Often, an offensive rebounder with several unopposed strides toward the basket can generate more momentum and consequently leap higher as he or she moves toward the ball. A quick, effective screen negates this attempt of the unopposed offensive rebounder.

Off-the-ball rebounding demands much more movement, as the distance between the defensive rebounder and the offensive rebounder can vary from several feet to fifteen or more feet. The backline defensive rebounder must take up much of this slack so the contact and position from basket allows for the proper body angle and recovery.

The Center or Post Defensive Rebounding

The problems of defensive rebounding are substantial if the proper mechanics of defensive rebounding are not applied. Because of the proximity of the defensive post rebounder to his or her opponent, it is necessary for he defensive post rebounder not only to immediately screen the opponent but to move into this rebounder with a low stance and the arms held upward. If possible, the defensive post rebounder should also move this offensive rebounder slightly away from the basket. The opponent's size, strength and weight will often cause the defensive rebounder to move to an ineffectual defensive position— i.e., standing under the basket.

As a result, the defensive player will have to jump up and backwards to rebound. This backward movement will often be employed to compensate for any size advantage the opponent may have. In reality, however, it is very difficult to leap if the body is going backward. Because basketball is described as a game of incidental contact, this kind of contact is permitted, assuming it isn't excessive. This interpretation refers to a description by Dr. Henry C. Carlson, a famous Pittsburgh coach of decades ago who was responsible for its inclusion into basketball's rule book. It replaced Dr. Naismith's original description that basketball is a non-contact sport. Dr. Carlson was appalled at the ticky-tac rebounding calls that were being called. The changed wording reduced fouls on rebounding by a great degree. It's another example of how important coaches are and have been to the constant growth and popularity of basketball. Imbalances must be identified and corrected. Always remember, the game of basketball is an inexact science. It needs constant monitoring.

The Do's and Don'ts of Rebounding

Do's

- Proper technique of the defensive rebounder demands a low, comfortable stance with arms extended upward at the shoulder level.
- The defensive rebounder should jump up and toward the ball to prevent the possibility of a strip or the opponent knocking the ball loose.
- As the defender descends with the recovery, the ball should be tightly held away from the body and the elbows out for protection.
- The defensive rebounder should land in a low stance with the ball protected as described in the previous point.
- The defensive rebounder should be conscious of the physical pressure, or lack of it, as he or she descends to floor. With no pressure, the defensive rebounder should immediately look for an outlet to commence offensive transition. If he or she is physically challenged, however, the defender should try to get the ball safely out of the basket-area congestion.
- Long rebounds should often be treated as the initiation of the transition game; and, if possible, the ball should quickly be advanced upcourt.

Don'ts

- Don't release too soon from a defensive screen.
- Don't allow your defensive rebounder to be moved forward because of a high stance.
- Don't allow a defensive rebounder to be lax in his or her responsibilities; one careless defender can cause the entire defensive-rebounding unit to break down.
- When coming down with the ball after rebounding it, don't expose it for a possible strip by the offensive rebounder.
- Don't bring the ball to your body after rebounding it.
- Don't expose the ball to your opponents in the basket area without using your arms and elbows to protect it.
- Don't carry your arms low when in a defensive rebounding stance since they can be easily pinned to your side by the heavy traffic in the basket area.

Summary—Rebounding

Several parallels exist between good solid individual defense and individual rebounding. If one defender in a team defense goes individual and doesn't fulfill team responsibilities, the defense breaks down. If one individual rebounder breaks down and allows easy access to the offensive rebound, two negatives may result—either an easy tap-in for two points or a follow-up that creates defensive rebounding problems for all of the teammates as each tap pushes the defender closer to basket and into a less-effective position should the defender gain the rebound. This stripping action occurs often in such a situation. Having lost the rebound angle, the defensive rebounder is leaping straight up and coming straight down. It is often the second tap that results in the basket, even more than the original tap. The surest way to avoid the second tap is by not allowing the first tap. Coaches should keep in mind that defensive rebounding involves proper technique, proper position, and proper protection of the rebound.

Drills should be employed throughout the season to emphasize the importance of good rebounding. Because slippage often occurs due to neglect, coaches should physically review the essential mechanics of sound rebounding throughout the season.

CHAPTER 7

OFFENSE COMPLEMENTING DEFENSE

No one word in basketball has more connotations than the word balance. It is used to describe a team's shooting abilities. It relates to spacing or balancing the court. It describes a team's ability concerning its offensive and defensive capabilities. It details the relative status of a team's strength on the floor concerning how well the playing personnel has both the ability to score and the capacity to defend individuals. It's closely associated with successful shooting, lateral movement and the recovery of a defender. Probably its the most important connotation refers to an offense that complements and balances a team's transition to defense.

For whatever reason, one of the earliest fundamentals a coach used to hear at clinics was, "Balance your offense and your defense." Having your offense complement your defense was traditionally a common theme at most clinics. Seldom, if never, did a clinician not spend part of the lecture on the concept that "your offense must complement your defense." I doubt today if one in twenty clinicians even brings up the subject. Has the game changed that much? Doesn't the defense begin when the opponent first has ball possession? Isn't the opponent then on offense? Isn't the theory of defending the ball first pretty much accepted by the great majority of coaches? To repeat, it isn't baseball or football which have a time interval between offense and defense. Why, then, isn't it treated more seriously today, especially when critical defensive problems of defending transition, the fast break and especially the three-point shot are considered. Shouldn't some thought be given to a defined transition from offense to defense—particularly as it relates to the opponent who has rebounded the offensive team's shot?

This important part of the game involving transition situations is termed as having an offense that complements the defense. This offense will rebound with a design that forms a triangle of rebounders in the basket area. The two low rebounders will be the post, whose responsibility is the low strongside of the triangle, and the low rebounder on the weakside who rebounds on the weakside under part of the triangle. The strongside wing player goes to the foul line, but not below. The two guards are spaced slightly above the foul-line circle and to the side. Basically, it is a balanced 2-1-2 situation for the shooting team, as the conversion to defense commences should the opponent rebound the ball.

Wherever the rebound angles, the two players of the triangle off the ball retreat in a straight line at top speed to the other paint area of the court. The foul-line rebounder should angle, should a low rebounder of the triangle contest the rebound, but not over-angle to the strongside to defend the strongside passing lane. The weakside retreater frontline angles toward the middle. The rebounder whose opponent has retrieved the missed shot is closely overplayed slightly toward the near sideline but positioned to be able to defend a dribble.

I prefer that frontline people play a denial defense on their immediate opponents without responsibility to pick up someone sprinting down court. I have always believed and practiced this theory. Football has reinforced the validity of such a premise. The rebounder covering the opponent rebounding the ball has defined responsibilities. The defender should not overcommit and lose position that would allow the rebounder to be able to turn and throw an unpressured pass downcourt or have a dribbling lane that can allow a drive un-opposed to the opposite end. The defender's responsibility is to keep a close position on the rebounder that does not allow a front turn for upcourt vision and space to throw an unopposed pass.

Pressure on the ball handler should be the first step in defensive transition. The other two rebounders who are sprinting full speed to the other end should have ball vision. The transition or break-point possibility should be diffused by the ball pressure. As has been seen over and over again, when an excellent passer in football completes pass after pass against a prevent defense, this same passer does not perform nearly as well when faced with defensive pressure. Under aggressive pressure, a passer is more likely to respond with incomplete passes, interceptions, sacks and occasional fumbles. The same premise prevails in basketball.

This example is another instance of a team being defensively complete because all elements of play are defended. This complementing theory is not a press defense but a normal system of play throughout the game. The defense is not attempting to focus on a steal but is alert for a forced or careless pass. Once the break or transition threat is ended, the defender hustles back on defense at least to the line of the ball or to the normal half-court defense area and picks up his or her assigned opponent in that area.

In part-method teaching, the mechanics are explained and taught. The post responsibility is explained to whoever is at the post position. Positioned at the foul line, the strongside wing player will contest and use the same method of playing the opposing rebounder as was outlined for the two lower triangle people. The weakside rebounder on offense has the duties of the other low rebounder, the post player.

It must be clearly stated to the players that this is not a press defense. It could be a manner of starting a press defense, but we have found it too confusing. What it is is a response to an opponent who can run better than our team that is designed to take away this part of their up-tempo game. It will depend on each player physically and mentally making this transition after the shot and ball recovery. The defender neither concedes the rebound nor overcommits. Because each position is well-defined, when a breakdown occurs, it can be pinpointed. If you have a flat tire, you don't put up the hood and mess with the carburetor. A coach must be able to identify breakdowns so that they can quickly be addressed.

A more perfect example of an offense complementing the defense could not exist than in today's NBA game. It has been stated and restated that a coach should examine rules, especially new ones, and make these rules work to the coach's advantage. Also, defensive strategy has always embraced the thought that lines of a court are allies of the defense. For example, the ten-second line is the cause of much defensive thought; the sideline invites trap thinking; the three-second area (for other reasons) is an ally of the defense. It has been difficult to understand why the clock couldn't give tactics to the defensive coach. Until recently, few coaches gave the game time clock much thought. However, in the NBA, Pat Riley has been given credit for his ingenuity of defensively using the 24-second clock to a real defensive advantage.

In the NBA, the 24-second clock is sacrosanct. It is the one rule that has been adopted throughout the world of basketball, but in different forms. In the NBA, it is 24 seconds; in the FIBA game, it is 30 seconds, and in the college and (more recently) at the high school level, it is 35 seconds. It was creative thinking that exposed the 24-second clock in its present form as being a detriment, rather than an asset, to an exciting game. The three-point shot has been suggested to be the villain, but it is merely the result, not the cause.

The following is a scenario where the offense can complement the defense. The defense picks up the ball close to the top of the circle on the backcourt. The backline is in a denial position to discourage the pass forward. The strategy at the distance is to try to keep the ball in the backcourt by good positioning on the ball for eight seconds. When the ball passes the midline, it is to be directed to a sideline with the backline in a tight denial, but not overextended. Another six or eight-seconds of pressure delays the offense the proper spacing for the commencement of their offense. At this point, the sideline defensive pressure eases somewhat and allows wing entry. The post player is allowed a low post with the defender behind the post player. The wing passes to the low-post player. Simultaneously with the pass, the second defender, usually the weakside frontline defender, whose job is to take away the post-player's move toward the paint area, doubles-down. The post defender overplays the baseline side because of topside help. When the post player gets the ball, only approximately eight seconds are left on the 24-second clock. While the post has the ball in a low position, the aggressive double team reduces the offensive potential in most instances. The remaining three defenders can legally zone the four outside players with a 3-player zone. The usual tactic for the 3-player zone is to invite the pass to the weakest perimeter shooter. This player will have time for an unhurried shot and maybe one pass to a hurried shooter to beat the 24-second clock.

The point of this scenario involves the four well-spaced offensive players—two at the wing and two on each side and behind the foul-line circle. When the shot is taken, the two offensive wing people retreat straight down each sideline. The two outside offensive players converting to defense then retreat to the vicinity of the midcourt circle. When the opponent retrieves the shot—made or rebounded, the ball is thrown to the outlet. The outlet gets the ball for transition offense. The four opponents are either over the midline or near it, and the strongside passing lane is closed by the retreating wing player. The converting-to-defense team uses the same tactics of delaying the ball into the normal half-court spacing. The result is an alarming number of 70-point games or less. However, the example shows how the offense can complement the defense.

What is the answer? One possibility would be for the high school, college, or FIBA not to adopt the 24-second clock as it is now used. However, I believe that if the clock commenced as soon as the ball was in the front court, the 24-second clock could then commence. This approach would allow the post player to reset the position to a higher area, as the additional seconds on the clock for the offense would allow a great deal of offensive cutting to the basket. This step could unclog the logjam the present situation creates, since little or no movement occurs when the post player is doubled—just spaced outside. The time problem and the defensive post player in the vicinity of the basket also discourage going to the basket without the ball when the low-posting offensive player has the ball. The three-point shot is the victim, since time doesn't permit much else.

This situation is an extreme example when describing how the offense should complement the defense. Red Holzman and his New York Knicks of the '70s were great practitioners of this type of conversion, but for different reasons. This quick four-player retreat kept scores low, since the Knicks were tough to run against, and it also led to two Knick NBA championships.

CHAPTER 8

TRANSITION DEFENSE

If this book has one consistency, it is the importance of adapting to new rules changes. Often a rule that could otherwise be considered an offensive rule creates more problems defending the change than improving a coach's offensive philosophy. A recent example of what I am suggesting was the adoption of the three-point shot rule. While it has had a large impact on offensive thinking and use by our high school and college coaches, as well as coaches in the NBA, its defensive implications are significant if a coach is to adjust his or her thinking to better defend the three-point shot.

A case in point was Coach Bob Knight and his Indiana program. Like many coaches, he privately and, I might add, publicly, voiced his opposition to this rule change. His main concern was the imbalance between the value of the ball and the penalty of the foul. It's an important, delicate balance about which coaches should always be concerned. In this instance, the three-point shot enhanced the value of the ball significantly. Fortunately, the rules committee recognized the imbalance and increased the penalty of the foul by a second foul shot when the tenth foul has been committed. Usually, the team that decides upon an offense that features the three-point shot will often shoot fewer foul shots since it shoots over the defense and doesn't rely on an attacking inside-type offense.

Coach Knight wisely concluded that it was a valid rule and one of which he would have to make the best use that his personnel would allow. Conversely, some coaches publicly and privately voiced their displeasure and stated that they would not change or adjust to it. Some were soon unemployed; others are still trying to recover programs that were successful before the three-point rule adoption but are not nearly as successful today. Coach Knight wisely used a great outside shooting guard, Steve Alford, and a squad that was predicted to be in the midpack of the Big Ten to earn an NCAA championship. He still doesn't like the rule, but he respects the impact it can have on the outcome of a game and a season.

I'm not sure if basketball coaches realize how much they can learn from other sports. Soccer, for example, teaches us the importance of ambidexterity of the feet. Soccer players must dribble and pass (soccer style) with either foot. Similarly, in basketball, the players' feet are used constantly throughout the game. As such, the ambidexterity of the feet is particularly important in the offensive aspects of the game. American football has borrowed many of basketball's basic concepts and principles in football's passing game. Isolation, flooding zone with proper spacing, moving screens, splitting the middle of two defenders who are switching are examples of techniques employed by many NFL teams in their passing game today. Coach Bill Walsh, the highly successful coach of the San Francisco 49ers in the late 1980s and early '90s, has often stated that he learned many of his offensive football principles from basketball. His impact on the passing game in the NFL is still the ruling thought with many of the more currently successful, winning NFL coaches.

I believe football has taught many of us the importance of ball pressure. As football coaches have learned from us, we can learn from them. We often see, at all levels of play, aggressive, active defensive football units that completely dominate an opponent featuring an exceptional passer and heretofore effective passing attack. For the better part of the game, the aggressive, physical defense has throttled the opponent, enabling the defensive squad's team to be comfortably ahead. In the fourth quarter, however, a defensive change occurs. The team then goes from aggressive, denial defense to a passing-soft defense, the so-called "prevent defense." The same passer who has until then been inept now becomes an accurate, positive passer. At that point, the dominated opponent becomes the dominant aggressor. Too often, a comfortable lead is nearly lost, or lost entirely.

Trying to recover the aggressive dominance the defense has had can be very difficult to do. Why? It's difficult to maintain a positive and aggressive attitude, but it can be done. To allow an aggressive, successful defense to become passive, and then attempt to recover the aggressive and confident bearing it initially had is nearly impossible. The point I am making is of the importance of pressuring the ball handler, which will invariably reduce his or her passing options and accuracy.

Defense should start when the opponent has the ball—both mentally and physically. This conversion is often under different circumstances. An opponent's defensive rebound, a made basket, an interception by the opponent, a loose ball recovery by the opponent, and a stolen dribble are the usual events associated with change of possession. In some of these instances, it is less difficult to immediately pressure the ball than in others. What is important is an immediate recognition defensively of this change of possession and a quick reaction to it in an organized manner.

Communication and a quick pickup of the opposing ball handler are of paramount importance. Drills that practice this immediate change will acquaint players with the proper responses to these varying situations. Some coaches use a whistle. Others vocally signify this conversion change in a practice scrimmage. In this type of scrimmage, the ball handler will immediately drop the ball to the floor and convert (as do his or her teammates also) to defense. The ball handler does not pick up the opponent who had been defending the ball but the nearest other opponent. In any conversion defense, loud communication is a must. Until a way is invented to score without the ball, it will always be the first reaction of the converting team to defense to pick up the ball.

Mechanics Of Fast Break And Transition Defense

It has been stated that basketball is a continuous action game. It needs constant attention to maintain the balances that are so necessary to keep it the game of action we have associated with it.

I have never felt there is only one way to play or coach basketball. If that ever happens, the creativity that has always been associated with the game and its coaches will be lost. The ability of its players to create and express their individualities will likewise be lost. The "system" that must always prevail, even at the expense of player development, is something of which we must always be aware. While creativity must stay within the parameters of the team's offense or defense, coaches should always allow for creativity in their offensive and defensive theories. The trend of the game that has bothered me most is that basketball is too often over-coached and under-taught.

An example has been given of how an offense can complement their defense against the fast break and transition basketball. It's up to the coach to decide what best suits the team's needs. Offensive rebounding, fewer trips to the foul line, a slow game tempo, and a stand-around offense are the results of this type of defensive counter to an up-tempo offense. Other coaches don't wish to give up their offensive movement, attacking the defense, getting to the foul line more frequently, and offensive rebounding. Again, as coaches, we have choices, and these choices must recognize team personnel and their capabilities and the opponent's strengths and weaknesses.

I preferred to solve the transition problem in another manner. As I have explained, I wanted to complement my defense with an offense geared to convert immediately to defense upon a loss of the ball through a missed shot, and to be positioned to immediately pressure the opponent who has recovered the rebound. From that point, we detailed the individual responsibilities until we assumed our normal half-court defense. I felt we were able to maintain our offensive rebounding abilities; we were able to immediately stall the progress of the ball upcourt by an aggressive individual response of our defenders and stay totally within our concepts of defensive ball pressure and aggressiveness.

Among the steps in our transition from offense to defense are the following:

- Offensive triangle of rebounding by the three inside players.
- Positioning the outside guards slightly behind and to the side of the foul-line circle.
- The rebounder in the immediate vicinity of the opponent's rebound recovery pressures his or her defensive rebounder with the purpose of preventing this rebounding opponent from being able to execute a front turn and to survey the entire court. The pressure should be close but not aggressive enough to cause a foul. Should the opponent attempt to rid himself or herself from the pressure by the use of a dribble, the lateral use of feet should maintain the defensive pressure on this rebounder.

- The two remaining triangle rebounders immediately convert to defense when they see the opponent's rebound recovery. They proceed to the opposite end of the court with the foul-line rebounder angling slightly strongside in the retreat and the weakside rebounder also in a straight-line retreat with a slight angle to the middle. Should the ball be rebounded by an opponent in the foul-line area, the top of the triangle rebounding trio executes the same pressure and tactics of the inside rebounders. In this case, the two low triangle rebounders return in straight lines with partial vision on the ball and slant toward the side should the ball be advanced up the sideline. Partial vision of the ball is important when retreating, since it will allow for a quick reaction should the opponent attempt a long up-court pass. Ball vision is always an important factor in all types of defense.

- The perimeter players have defined responsibilities. They pick up their immediate opponent and deny the outlet pass. If the outlet receiver is forced to go toward the baseline, this defender has done his or her job. The entire purpose of this type of defense is to slow the progress of the ball upcourt, not necessarily to intercept the pass. The weakside defender should tightly deny a pass to the middle in the event that the initial outlet pass is completed. Once it has been determined that the fast break or transition offense has been contained, these frontline defenders retreat to the normal defensive areas of their basic halfcourt defense. This defense must not be confused with the press defense. Their purposes and responsibilities are entirely opposite. The above-described defense is a defense of containment and retarding the progress of the ball from the backcourt to the forecourt. The press defense, as it has been described, is an aggressive, denial, pressuring-type of defense that hopes to create turnovers and interceptions. It is very important to describe the "why" of these various defenses. When the players comprehend the "why" of the execution, the improvement in deploying the various defenses will be very evident.

- When the initial impetus of the opponent's fast break has been blunted and the flow of the ball upcourt has been stemmed, the defense should retreat to the normal defensive responsibilities of their half-court defense.

Summary—Transition Defense

Two examples have been presented of defending the fast break and transition offenses that will be successful if properly executed. While they are totally opposite in theory, both are effective. In reality, other means of trying to control tempo exist. The point that I want coaches to fully understand is that what best suits the strengths and limitations of a team's personnel, what conforms to the basic concepts of the coach and keeps his or her theory consistent with other principles of defensive play should be the guiding basis for the defensive team to adopt a particular theory. A coach should never adopt a style of play because another team and coach has had great success with the particular scheme of play unless it conforms to the concepts of the coach. Coaches should be flexible in thought and concept, so that they can borrow styles of play that others have had success with—but only these styles are within the aforementioned parameters of their concepts.

"Coach what you know and know what you coach" is a good axiom to follow, but don't be ignorant of how you can improve your knowledge and your team's play. Coaches should never allow themselves to be dogmatic and to reject a successful style of play without examining how they could possibly adopt that type of play into their total thoughts of acceptable play. Dogmatism has been the bane of many basketball coaches. Avoid it!

Defensive Retreat Situations

In my opinion, an inviolable rule is for a defensive player to retreat at full speed to the line of the ball. This imaginary line is one that runs from sideline to sideline through the axis of the ball. This retreat should extend to at least the foul line, and slightly below if the ball is advanced by the opponent to the baseline of the offense. It is to be presumed that when the opponent is on defense, the defenders are between the offense and the basket. Should the shooting team's outside man take off while the ball is in the air, the shooting team plays each defender individually. Accordingly, when their opponents take off, they go with them. The safety player of this defense is often the foul-line rebounder unless his or her opponent rebounds the ball. The other two inside rebounders sprint back in straight lines, and in a sense they are the safety players.

In this transition from being the offensive team to being on defense as the opponent captures the rebound, each player in his or her defensive transition has his/her responsibilities. If a breakdown occurs that allows for frequent baskets by the opponent, it is easily discernible by the coach. It is very important that coaches are able to ascertain problems and to identify where the breakdown occurs. With defined responsibilities, coaches can pinpoint a team's breakdowns and work to correct them. Assigned responsibilities allow for these corrections. Never has transition been more effective or important than in today's game. The threat of the three-point shooter demands that the defense be organized to pressure the initial offensive ball handler, but also to keep up pressure until this initial threat is lessened by a full-contesting defense with ball pressure. Covering the strongside, sideline passing lane is of utmost importance to discourage long passes to open receivers on the ball-side. As the players better understand their responsibilities, they will improve as a unit and gain confidence in their ability to control a team that depends upon the quick up offense.

Teams that are well matched with an opponent usually win or lose because they can or can't control the tempo of the game. The tempo of the game of basketball can best be determined by the defense, not the offense. Time and again, this proves to be true.

If there is one defensive situation that brings out an emotional response by the coach, it is a defensive player in retreat running at half speed when the ball is well ahead of the player up the court. Because this defender's assigned opponent is behind him or her, this slow retreat may be acceptable to the defensive player—but few coaches would agree. Centers are usually the culprits in this situation. Because I have many NBA and college centers at my Big Man camps, I address this problem with a very simple drill. Constantly exhorting our players to retreat full speed to the line of the ball yet not getting the results I desired, I made my point with the following drill:

> Two players are employed at a time in drill. The player with the ball is a very active player with the quickness and ability to drive to the basket. He is guarded by a center—a slower-moving player. The player with the ball is positioned about 30 feet from the basket at a point about 10 feet from the sideline. I stand in the back court about 20 feet away and pass the ball to the quick, active, smaller player. I tell the center to guard him on a one-on-one situation. Obviously, the quicker player easily beats him going right and going left. The center isn't too happy that it's such a mismatch. After this point is firmly entrenched in the center's mind, another player is added to the drill. This additional player is a second defensive player who sprints full speed to the receiver and cuts off the drive to the middle. The slower center now has help to the middle, so he overplays the sideline side and is able to prevent being beaten on a drive up the inside line.

The purpose of this drill is to visibly demonstrate the importance of a full-speed defensive retreat by all players—particularly by the center. Often, the passing center will lumber upcourt at half speed. This enables the retreating defensive player or center to help his or her teammate guard an opponent who has the ball with a lot of court for the ball handler to work with and a defensive player to defend. Full speed retreat will, to a great degree, eliminate this type of defensive problem.

Summary—Defensive Retreat Situations

Offensively, coaches constantly strive for the advantage of numbers, e.g., 3-on-2, 2-on-1, overloading a side in attacking a zone, and by good spacing, even creating an open shot when the numbers are 5-against-4. Why then isn't the same thinking applied to defense? Good rules of defensive retreat will often give the defense this same advantage if its quick retreat gives it a numerical advantage.

Drill situations should be created that give the players a visible picture, not just a word picture, of what point the coach is trying to stress. Once the player has a visible picture, a verbal reminder by the coach will have a greater impact.

The rule of full-speed retreat to the line of the ball makes a team defense complete in a sense. The ball or the ball handler is the most important opponent to be concerned with, not the opponents in the backcourt when the ball is in the opponent's forecourt. This point should always be strongly emphasized by the coach, again stressing how teammates can and should help each other on defense. It's another great example of the "we" and "us" concept as it applies to defense.

The Three-on-Two Situation

When three offensive players who are properly spaced in transition basketball have outnumbered the two defenders, basically two ways exist for the defense to react:

- *The tandem defense by the two defenders.* This type of formation by two defenders in the three-on-two transition situation has been the most common and accepted defensive spacing in basketball since fast-break basketball was first introduced. Fundamentally, it determines the exact responsibilities of each of the two defenders. The top player of the tandem is charged with contesting the ball; the lower defender in the tandem assumes a zone-type responsibility and guards the basket area. Should the ball be passed to either wing from the passer who is in the foul-circle area, the back defender of the tandem picks up the ball receiver, while the top defender of the tandem positions in the middle of the paint area and zones the basket area. Should the wing passer now return a pass to the original passer who is in the vicinity of the foul line, the tandem adjusts to its original position with the defender who has picked up the wing cutter with the ball returning to his or her original position in the paint and defending the basket. The original top defender who had retreated to the zone position in the basket area then picks up the ball at the foul line. Simply, the ball, theoretically, is always covered and pressured, and the other two offensive wing players without the ball are being zoned by the lower tandem player. Again, it is a delaying tactic until help for the two defenders returns to the line of the ball.

- *The lateral or side-by-side, two-player defense.* This type of formation has become a more popular defensive reaction since the advent of the three-point shot. The tandem defense has a problem creating any real pressure on the wing player who spots up at the three-point line. The distance from the middle of the paint area to a position of defending or bothering the spotted up three-point shooter is too far for effective pressure on the shooter. The lateral defense, adhering to a rule of retreat that demands only one foot in the paint area, allows for a more effective closing of the spotted-up shooter at the three-point line. Further, today's high school and college coach emphasizes outside shooting and recruits more outside shooters. Prior to the adoption of the three-point shot, coaches, for the most part, favored more athleticism, jumping, and inside players. While a need will always exist for the inside player, this change of thinking has caused more inclusion of the less-talented but more-effective long-range shooter who can stretch the defense. It's another example of coaches recognizing that new rules or interpretations can cause a rethinking of playing personnel and types of offenses and defenses that will best serve them or their teams as they adjust to these new rules.

Rotation Defense

Some coaches term rotation as "fool's gold." It looks a lot better than it actually is. In spite of its weaknesses, it is nevertheless an important facet of good team defense. We call it the last vestige of team defense. Simply, rotation is an important team defensive mechanism for a team to use in the proper circumstances. It is a "help" part of team defense that involves a nearby team member picking up a drive to the basket or an open opponent who is intending to shoot an otherwise open shot.

The strengths of a rotation defense are to contest the open opponent who has eluded his or her assigned defender. Without the help of the nearby defender, this offensive player will have an uncontested lay-up or a high percentage face-up shot. Rotation should allow the defense to perform one of the most important tenets of good defense—have pressure on the ball.

The weaknesses of a rotation defense are the problems caused by four defensive teammates executing the rotation simultaneously—and the ensuing mismatch situations that often occur. The defensive post player is often the defender who must first initiate the rotation process. When this defender leaves his or her assigned opponent, mismatches often occur. A weakside back defender now rotates to the bigger offensive center, and the rotation of the front, weakside defender must slide down to pick up the much bigger (in most instances), weakside offensive forward. The other frontline defender must defend the two offensive frontline opponents at the perimeter. This process is the normal defensive rotation when an offensive wing player drives baseline past the defender who is charged with defending this player.

Obviously, the rotation process is necessary if an unopposed shot is not to occur. It is important that a coach walk through this entire rotation process to impress each defender that one careless individual defender can break down team defense and often cause a teammate to risk a foul by the mismatches that occur on the easy offensive putback or rebound that rotation often permits. This scenario often happens also when a frontline defender reaches around behind the offensive opponent who has dribbled past the defender and is proceeding toward the basket. It's nothing more than a last-ditch effort by a defender who has depended upon his or her hands rather than the feet.

Some situations exist in which some coaches feel a rotation defense is the best applicable defense. For example, an extremely talented offensive player is isolated on a defender who is not physically capable of stopping the offensive player from penetrating the defense. Teammates must be alert to double this talented offensive player who has beaten the less-talented defender. It's a mismatch situation.

What is really important is how this rotation defense is presented to the team—its strengths and its weaknesses—when it could be termed a permissible defense, and when it is covered by the individual breakdown of a selfish defender, a lazy defender or a mentally incompetent defender. I believe the principles of the rotation defense are a "must" for any team. However, a rotation defense should be considered, in most instances, the last vestige of team defense.

The "WHY" of the Shell Defense

The transition from offense to defense occurs for a variety of reasons. A rebound by the opponent, an errant pass, a loose ball, a made shot, and an interception are the principal reasons for the change. In some instances, the offense has some time in making the transition to defense. In other instances, it is immediate and unexpected. Because the transition to defense in these situations finds the defense spread over the court, the immediate cohesion of the defense is difficult. Few teams practice a plan to best handle this transition.

The shell defense is a defense that can bridge the need for transition where the defense by immediately reading and reacting to the situation has a chance to delay the offense that is attempting to take advantage of a numerical advantage that often is the case when a turnover—e.g., an interception, a loose ball or a careless protection of the ball—occurs. To quickly assemble a shell or triangle defense, communication is really important. The player closest to the ball should communicate loudly that he or she has defense on the ball. The other two defenders quickly assemble the triangle. In any defense, picking up the ball is the first priority of a team defense. Preventing two people from picking up the ball and leaving an opponent free can only be accomplished by communication. Often, no one picks up the ball, if there is no vocal call of "ball."

On occasion, a tandem of two defensive players facing three or more offensive players can adjust to a quick shell or triangle as the third defender returns to the basket area. In some instances, this returning defender can assume the top of the triangle position, while the top player of the tandem rotates to the weakside of the lower part of the triangle. A level of flexibility must exist that will allow for rotation, but will ensure that a defender will always be positioned to pressure and pick up the ball.

When the opponent has ball possession, defense begins for the other team. Mentally, defense should immediately commence. Physically, it is logical to prepare a team to immediately position themselves to prevent an easy basket. The basic purpose of the shell is to prevent an easy lay-up. It is a delaying defense that is spaced to pressure the ball handler or shooter. It is not an exact, planned-type defense because of the quick need to assemble but with no exact, preconceived floor position. In defending a fast break or transition, the shell is the wedge between a normal defense and a retreating defense that has its front defenders behind the ball. When the front defenders have returned to the perimeter defense positions, the shell dissolves into the normal five-player defense. Because the shell is actually a three-player zone defense, it is important that the return to the normal defense from the shell is accompanied by a loud vocal call of "normal" or some such identification of the basic defense of their team. The player defending the ball as his or her teammates reassemble to their normal defense stays on the ball regardless of the mismatch. The ball should never be left unguarded in the forecourt.

Mechanics of the Shell Defense

Defenses cannot properly or effectively operate with fewer than the five players. There is an interdependence of a defensive unit that precludes it being efficiently productive without all five players addressing themselves to their individual responsibilities. The shell defense is an integral part of the total individual responsibility when defending the fast break in a transition situation.

The shell defense is a 3-player defense used when the offense has penetrated the outer perimeter of the defense and has gained a numerical advantage over the defense (e.g., a four-to-three ratio favoring the offense.) The defense in this instance is usually poorly spaced and apparently disorganized as to responsibilities. Often the defense will immediately pick up the closest offensive player. However, the defense being outnumbered, an uncovered opponent flashes to the basket unopposed and catches a pass for an easy, unguarded basket. The shell defense is designed to prevent this easy basket. Communication is the heart of any team. It is particularly important when unexpected situations arise. In this instance of being outnumbered four to three, the first of the three defensive men to recognize the situation loudly communicates *"shell."* The three defensive players deploy themselves quickly in a 3-man triangle zone with the top player in the triangle retreating to a position several feet above the foul line. The two near men station themselves close to the basket but with only one foot placed in the paint area. This factor is important. If the back players get both feet in the paint, they are vulnerable to an open 3-point shot. With one foot, they can create pressure to this 3-point shot and still go against the drive for a lay-up. This shell defense is only a 2- or 3-second defense since the front-line defensive players should retreat at full speed to the vicinity of the 3-point line on either side of the foul-line circle. When the front defensive players have reached this position, the top defensive men of the triangle-shell defense should communicate loudly "normal defense." At this point, what was momentarily a 2-1-2 zone becomes a normal man defense as each individual picks up the closest man. In event of a mismatch, all players should be alert for a switch to minimize the mismatch problems, but never leave the ball unguarded. Usually, the offense has to reassemble in their spacing so the defensive readjustment is not a real problem. A zone defense can make its adjustment when the *normal* communication is given. Consistency is very important in every phase of the game. Communication is all-important in defense. If the defense can prevent the easy lay-up when it is pressuring the opponent and still be positioned to hurry the outside shot, it will be a winning and effective defense. The shell defense is the middle part of a press or a defense against the fast break or transition, as the opponent tries to take advantage of its numbers. The shell is between the front pressure and the usual half-court normal defense.

It is important for a defense to be totally in tune with one another in every situation. No "loose ends" should exist that are left to chance. When the players' responsibilities are defined, the chance for "loose ends" is minuscule. If a defense is patiently explained and taught, the players will better understand its markings and more effectively employ it. Without loud communication, it can lose its effectiveness.

Transition has never been more effective or important than in today's game. The threat of the three-point shooter demands that the defense be organized to pressure the initial offensive ball handler and to keep this pressure on until this initial threat is lessened by a full-contesting defense with ball pressure. Covering the strongside, sideline passing lane is of utmost importance to discourage long passes to open receivers on the ball side. As the players better understand their responsibilities, they will improve as a unit and gain confidence in their ability to control a team that depends upon the quick-up offense.

Teams that are well matched with their opponents usually win or lose because they can or can't control the tempo of the game. The tempo of the game of basketball can best be determined by the defense, not the offense. Time and again, this factor proves to be true.

CHAPTER 9

THE PRESS DEFENSE

The greatest single area of improvement in basketball is the press defense. The game was over 50 years old before this defense made any significant impact upon the play of the game. Subsequently, it has become a true "amoeba" defense, as it takes on many faces and as many face changes.

As stated before, it was not conceived until after the elimination of the center jump in the late '30s. For any number of reasons, once the center jump was eliminated after each made basket, coaches were obsessed with important things other than basketball. The game was put on hold, in a sense, until World War II ended and the great number of coaches who were in the military returned to their coaching positions.

What really caused the initiation of this defense was the inversion concept. Guards were the defenders of the basket and the defensive rebound. Offensively, they brought the ball upcourt on offense. They did not invert as they do today. Some of the coaches (and I was one of them) tried the inversion concept in the late '40s. However, the press was not the purpose at the time. The purpose was to have size on both boards. Before inversion, the smaller frontline defenders were the offensive rebounders at the other end. The one area of concern was allowing a long pass downcourt with no real pressure on the opposing rebounder. The triangle theory of rebounding on the offensive board was necessary if the rebounder was to be harassed. The defensive rebounder had to be played tightly to prevent upcourt vision and a turn that would allow an unopposed outlet pass.

The pressure of the rebounder and the quick transition to defense by the other two offensive rebounders in the triangle created an opportunity for the smaller, quicker players who were the offensive guards to extend their defense to the backcourt of the opponent. Soon after the elimination of the center jump, a second new rule was enacted—the installation of the 10-second line. Simply, this meant a 3/4 or half-court press could easily be effective, since the offense must now attack the press in order to avoid the 10-second rule violation. The 10-second backcourt and midline rule stimulated much more thinking involving the inversion concept, the pressure on the defensive rebounder, and an offense that was complementary to the defense (i.e., the triangle of rebounding on the offensive board). The initial focal point of being able to invert and keep the taller and more effective rebounders on both boards was now extended to taking advantage of the speed and quickness of the defensive matchup in the opponent's backcourt. The smaller, quicker defenders created many ball-handling problems for the bigger, slower opponents who were bringing the ball upcourt from their own backcourt. It gave proof to the theory that a smaller team wants the game to be played in the vicinity of the midline but not in the basket area. The concept applied partially in this phase of the game. Soon inversion, if only for self-defense, became standard procedure—but not until the 1950s.

The National Invitational Tournament was the first national collegiate tournament. The NCAA was created in the late '30s, several years after the creation of the NIT. The NCAA was a closed tournament that invited only conference champions. The NIT invited all teams that had excellent records, particularly the independents. Although they lacked a conference affiliation, many of the independents were the best teams in the country. In the 1948-'49 NIT, the University of San Francisco team won the tourney; and the NCAA winner, Kentucky, was eliminated in its first N.I.T. tournament game. By the mid-'50s, not only had the NCAA allowed independents, it also enlarged its tourney from eight to sixteen teams. Eventually it expanded to the 64 teams, where it now comprises the most exciting and publicly-accepted of any tournament or championship played today in any sport. This entire growth was the blueprint of Walter Byers, who became executive director of the NCAA in the mid-'50s.

In the 1948-'49 NIT, the USF team had several real advantages, including the fact that they played the half-court press defense and inverted their players, thereby enabling them to use their quickness and size to a real advantage. As a result, they succeeded in holding their opponents to a much lower point total than was their normal game average. They were also able to diffuse the fast breaks and to create a tempo that was best suited to their style of play. USF was the rank outsider going into the tourney, but the confidence they had in their inversion and press defense allowed them to overcome any fear of an opponent.

The half-court press my teams used extended 10 to 12 feet from the midline into the opponent's backcourt. The purpose of this spacing was to allow the defense to be organized and positioned as their opponents advanced upcourt from their backcourt. Also, the area between the frontline of the defense to the backline was narrowed. This open area is the vulnerable area of a press, since the opponent usually uses this open area to release the pressure on the backcourt teammates bringing up the ball. In a full-court press, this area is much more difficult to defend. As the front players of a press pull back to the vicinity of the midline, however, this area narrows and is less vulnerable in this type of half-court press. In the evolution of the press defense, the various zone-type presses are designed to minimize this wide area between the front and the back of a full-court press defense.

As the inversion concept was becoming more popular and the press was given more thought, a rethinking of personnel needs became more and more evident. The smaller, quicker and more adept ball handlers were being given more attention as coaches assessed their team needs. The tall, less-agile, big players were becoming more valuable as the inversion concept relieved the bigger players of ball-handling and dribbling responsibilities in the backcourt. Defensive rebounders became more important as the success of the fast break depended on the outlet pass after the rebound.

Soon, the fast break became a very important staple of the game as the personnel demands changed. Probably the biggest cause for tempo change of the game was the emergence of the black player. Prior to 1950, relatively few black players were playing Division I basketball. In the early 1950s, only one black player was on a Big 10 team, only several on the Pacific Coast Conference teams, and none on Division I teams in the South. In the '50s, things changed. The University of San Francisco, which featured Bill Russell, Casey Jones and Hal Perry in their starting lineup, broke many racial barriers. This USF team won the NCAA in both 1955 and 1956. It also set a record of 60-plus consecutive wins. Their coach was Phil Woolpert, who had been my assistant at USF and who became the USF coach when I left to take over the Michigan State position. I might add that Phil was my close friend and teammate, prior to the war, at what is now Loyola-Marymount. The press defense had never been played better than by those great USF teams of the mid-'50s.

The quickness, speed, and athleticism that the black athlete brought to basketball allowed the press defense to take many forms. As team quickness improved, full-court presses were initiated to complement three-quarter court or half court presses. Conditioning became more important to coaches, as the full-court defensive press demanded great stamina and endurance. It made opponents who were less conditioned to become disorganized, which created easy baskets caused by their turnovers. Up-tempo coaches realized that the press could help create a more suitable tempo. More and more reasons surfaced for the use of the press. These many reasons are detailed later in this Chapter.

One of the early features of the press (and the main one actually) was the surprise element. The great increase of popularity and the usefulness of this defense soon diminished the surprise factor. The "amoeba" factor of the press became evident as coaches became more creative in the employment of their presses. The importance of the complementary factors in the use of various-type presses introduced in the past decade or more are an indication of its versatility.

As has been stated, USF's use of a half-court press in the 1949 NIT was an impetus for its acceptance, since it was the first team with a defense of this type to win a national title. In the mid-'50s, USF again, with the same type of press complemented by a zone-type defense, won the NCAA tournament championship twice. Furthermore, the University of California at Berkeley using the identical press, albeit different personnel, won the NCAA in the 1958-'59 season. In the mid-'60s, UCLA, featuring the full-court, zone-type press, won the first of its many NCAA titles. The Bruins press involved a pick-up at the baseline by their center, with the team in a 1-2-1-1 alignment. The back player was Keith Erickson, one of the truly great athletes of that time. Keith was a world-class volleyball player, who also eventually became an important member of the Laker NBA championship team of 1971. This team had a 6'6" center and no one else over 6'4". They had both quickness and the smarts, and were superbly conditioned. Coach John Wooden featured the press defense in each of his numerous NCAA titles. The real strength of the UCLA defense was its ability to change the alignment and still keep its aggressiveness and integrity. Its 1-2-1-1 became a 1-2-2 or a 1-3-1 as it adjusted to counter the opponent's initial strategy and plan of attack to their press. These UCLA teams complemented and adjusted their zone press better than any other press that has ever been seen. The latest practitioner of the press has been the successful Kentucky Wildcat teams that were coached by Rick Pitino and Tubby Smith. Theirs was a full-court, individual-type press with some switch situations and even zone responsibility. This is an example of the ability of the basic press to take different forms. In this situation, the press is designed to play the ball handler straight up, switch or double the ball on any crossing, and use zone tactics off the ball weakside. Some teams will start with a zone type 1-3-1 or 2-2-1 and switch to an aggressive individual-type defense.

As stated earlier, the creativity of today's coaches has extended the use of the press as a weapon. Its relationship to many NCAA championship teams from the late '40s to the present time is an indication of the flexibility of the press to be adjusted to new rules changes and personnel changes. It creates excitement for the public who follow and support the game. Its impact on the tempo of the game, the need of a team that is behind to manage more ball possessions in order to erase the opponent's score advantage, and the strategic and psychological impact it creates are valid reasons why every coach should study and find ways to embrace the many potentially positive factors of a press in determining a game's outcome. It must be noted, however, that speed and team quickness are important elements of the full or 3/4-type presses. A team lacking in real quickness can effect a half-court press that extends the backcourt but close to the midline. The more a press extends its frontline from the backline, the more important speed and quickness factors become.

THE PRESS DEFENSE

"The Why"

Of all the various team defenses played in basketball today, the *press* defense is the latest. The *man-to-man* defense was initially the popular defense at the inception of the game. This was followed by the *zone* defense in its many forms. The man-to-man defense was modified by the *switching* defense. The switching defense had considerable popularity prior to the war, particularly in the '30s. The 1941 NCAA champion, Stanford University, best exemplified the basic purpose of the switch defense—to minimize the dangers of a mismatch. The starting five of this Stanford team ranged between 6'3" and 6'5" and were of similar size and strength. A mismatch was no problem since their players were equally effective inside and out. The press defense had not yet made its debut.

It has often been noted that new rules are the originators in the game's changes. It usually takes several years until the coaches adopt a major rules change and adjust totally to a change of play. The rules prior to the elimination of the center jump didn't allow for a press defense to be feasible and certainly not to be effective. After each basket made, the ball was returned to the center circle at midcourt for a jump ball. Some teams would simulate an individual press on the rebounder, but it was more by chance than by plan. A further discouragement of the use of a press type of defense was the court itself.

As previously stated, the important rules changes in the late '30s created a different game from what was played prior to the adoption of these two new rules—the elimination of the center jump after each made basket and, soon after, the installation of the ten-second midcourt line. It was unfortunate that it actually took close to a decade before any real material change in basketball occurred. The principal reason was the disruption caused by World War II. Many coaches realized that the service draft might soon tap them on the shoulder. Because of this possibility, the coaching ranks were being depleted more and more each month by enlistments in branches of the service other than the Army. More important matters than basketball were on the minds of these coaches as war became more imminent. The game, in a sense, was put on hold.

In 1946, very few teams had previously employed an organized press defense. It was almost as if the game of basketball was being reborn, as not many coaches had given thought to their new game. They were products of the old game, both as players and later as coaches. Some teams, most notably Rhode Island State and Marshall College, were among the early practitioners of this new game. Scores climbed from the 40's and 50's to the 80's and above in some instances. It was a wonderful, creative time to coach because so many different theories of play were surfacing.

Many coaches were what could be called 'half-court coaches' and didn't believe in this new fast tempo. Theories were put to a real test as most coaches were, and are, products of what they had been taught, what they had read, and what collectively these experiences had caused them to believe in as the proper approach. Some coaches responded by changing to a game they really didn't know or understand. Others stood the test by adjusting to these new rules with a flexibility that was able to inculcate into their basic thinking and background a more upbeat game—but always with awareness of the value of ball possession and the disastrous effect turnovers can cause.

One thing was certain in this post-war period: coaches seldom saw the same offense two games in row. Being part of this change, I was taught that I must operate from a base of the fundamentals I had learned as a player and what I later taught before I entered the service. I discovered that I also had learned a flexibility of thought that allowed me to adapt to rules changes. I have found that any rules change of importance should be examined as to how it can help a coach. Some coaches resent rules changes and never adapt to them.

My first year of college coaching began in 1946, immediately upon my discharge from the Navy. I had enlisted in February of 1942 at Great Lakes, Illinois. It was my exposure to Midwest basketball, which was quite different in play when compared to West Coast basketball. I was a member of the Great Lakes team. It was a very strong team that played many Big Ten teams and the strong independents of the Midwest. It was a great learning experience. Previously, I had begun my coaching career, prior to enlisting in the Navy, at St. John's Military Academy in Los Angeles. The style of Midwest basketball was much different in philosophy from that of the West. It was a much faster-paced game in the Midwest with less emphasis on defense. The West was defense-minded and basically half-court offense in concept.

I was exposed to part-method teaching by a Midwest basketball legend, Coach Tony Hinkle. Tony was one of those coaches in the '20s and '30s who gave the game its early impetus and the direction we have all profited from in our coaching careers. Great Lakes had an extremely talented team, and I am sorry to report that I was not one of those really talented members. I was more devoted to learning how to teach and coach, since I had played little basketball prior to my military enlistment. I was, however, as a team member, exposed to a whole sea of different offensive and defensive concepts, and different teaching methods and techniques as we practiced and played the various teams in the Midwest. While I never saw any evidence of an organized press defense, I did see a faster-paced offensive game. It was a great learning experience for me, and I was forever grateful to Coach Hinkle, who taught me to break down my defensive concepts.

While basketball progressed in many areas in 1946, the inversion concept had not made any really noticeable inroads into the tactics of the game. The offensive guards were the bigger people other than the center, and the quicker and smaller players were the offensive forwards and frontline defenders. As I explained in the earlier chapter on transition defense, I gambled that I could invert and keep my big men on both boards and my smaller men as my offensive play-making guards and frontline defensive men. It sounds simple today, but in those early days while we tried to be creative, we also were conscious that we couldn't jeopardize our livelihood and profession for some idealistic concept that smarter coaches than we had not adopted.

Now that I had committed myself to this inversion concept, I was struck with the advantage it gave me defensively. I could force and press the ball in the backcourt with the advantage of speed and quickness over the size and strength of our bigger opponents in the backcourt. I believed, and still do, that if I have the speed and quickness advantage and the opponent has the size and strength advantage, then I want the game to be played in the midcourt area, not in the paint area. We were able to create real problems for teams that didn't invert.

On the strength of our developed press defense, we were able to parlay it into the 1949 NIT championship as we expanded our various employments of the press. Without inversion, it would have been very difficult to effectively use the press defense. I have never had reason to question my original concept that an effective press defense can complement the initial press with a second press.

The next section of this Chapter presents a description of the steps involved in our press defensive play.

The Coward's Press

I don't have any real reason for naming this as I did, except that we faked our pressure more than we made things happen. I have always subscribed to the theory that lines are the allies of the defense—the baselines, the sidelines, the 3-second area line, and certainly the midcourt 10-second line. I have always felt it was very important to be organized when positioned to employ the press. With this in mind, I wanted my frontline players about 10-12 feet in front of the midcourt line. We played the ball straight up between the ball handlers and basket, a slight slough to the middle by the weakside, frontline player and slightly back. Our backline was in a denial position strongside and on the offensive center. The weakside, backline player was in a weakside zone unless an opponent broke toward the ball; he would then contest. In a sense, we occupied the ball but not over aggressively; we contested leads but were conscious and aware of the back cut to which we could be we could be vulnerable. We had the bark but not really the bite.

It has been my contention that most coaches spend more time preparing against a press defense team than against any other factor in the game. I was always very interested in knowing what the opponent's plan was before we made any real commitment to our counter to the opponent's plan. Hence, the coward's press. Since we were able to learn their attack plan practically all the time, we made sure while employing this coward's press that we gave up practically nothing and learned a lot. It was very instrumental in our success in 1949. Since our counter press usually created real problems for an opponent, they would have trouble countering our counter to their game plan. Another real advantage that we had involved the fact that very few teams played the press, which created many problems for teams that had not encountered this type defense.

Basically, our counter defense was part zone, part switch, and part man. We planned to invite the opponents to different paths than in our initial press. In our initial press, we would give away the sideline. In our zone-type press, we would take that path away and force the dribble to the middle. In our initial press, we had a normal slough from the weakside guard. In our counter, we had a much longer slough toward the ball handlers, and we were close enough to knock the ball away if they tried to split our frontline players. The off-defensive guard would advance toward the ball handler laterally with his or her arms extended to present a problem should the dribbler attempt to pass laterally. The defender's main purpose is to influence the ball handler's pass to be angled away from the midcourt line. This tactic is designed to cause a time problem for the opponent needing to cross the 10-second line. Should this pass be in the vicinity of the 10-second line, the weakside, backline defender is anticipating the pass for a possible interception.

Rather than illustrate a particular press defense, I want to review the purposes of the press, the basic theory of its use, the importance for every team to be able to employ it when needed, and its relation to game tempo, strategy, and proper use of a particular type of personnel. It is important for a coach and the team to understand "why" it is being used, when it's best employed, and when to use it more aggressively—and when to back off and, in a sense, regroup.

"Why" the Press Defense?

- to create a tempo of play that best suits the team's personnel.
- to pressure poor ball-handling teams.
- to attack poorly-organized teams.
- to wear down poorly-conditioned teams.
- to disrupt the flair and fluidity of an opponent's normal offensive play.
- to take advantage of teams whose offenses are lateral with little or no diagonal or straight-line cutting.
- to take advantage of situations early in the season before some teams are prepared for a press.
- to use against a slower opponent.
- to employ against a bigger and less-active opponent.
- to create an aggressive, mental response at the beginning of an important game. (Often, teams that are playing really important games—e.g., state championship or tournament finals, conference or national championship must-win games—start the game negatively).
- to use when behind, particularly late in the game.
- to create preparation problems for an opponent. (Most coaches fear an opponent's press as it can disrupt the offensive game plan, and much preparation time of the opponent is spent on attacking the press).
- to distort the normal spacing of the opponent's offense.
- to take advantage of the skills of a veteran team that has the flexibility to adjust to unexpected counters of the opponent.
- to employ against an inexperienced opponent.

The press defense has more legitimate reasons for its use than any other single tactic of basketball. For the first half-century or more, the press defense was a seldom-used or taught method of play. Like many important changes that have occurred in basketball since the game's inception, its birth was another result of the important rules changes of the late '30s—the elimination of the center jump after each made basket, the adoption of the 10-second backcourt rule, and the installation of the center or midcourt line. The continuity of the game prior to these rules changes was of little importance to the rules makers of that time. A fast tempo game couldn't consistently happen prior to the late '30s because the ball was walked upcourt to the center circle after a made basket where a jump ball then occurred. Fast-break basketball only occurred when interceptions were made or loose-ball recoveries occurred. No one played a press defense as it was later adopted in the late '40s. Inversion was not known or practiced at that time.

Coaches were slow to invert their players immediately after the war. Necessity was eventually the principal reason for the acceptance of inverting as a tactic by coaches because the matchup problem of bigger, slower ball handlers being harassed by the smaller guards changed many coaches' thinking. The continuity of the game from the jump-ball rule to taking the ball out after a made basket gave the game an up-tempo it hadn't previously had. Many smaller teams became very competitive against an opponent with superior size but less quickness.

In 1950-51, my first year at Michigan State, our starting lineup averaged slightly over 6 feet one inch. Our center was only 6'4" but very active. We were able to stay competitive against the best of the Big Ten teams and occasionally win a game or two. We tried to force the game to be played in the midcourt, as opposed to around each basket. We could never have competed evenly against these same teams if we had played them straight up. The press defense, however, created enough turnovers and better use of our primary advantage—quickness—that we were able to stay in every game.

Whatever competitive advantages a team may have, a coach should try to find ways to exploit these advantages and attack what may be perceived as weaknesses of an opponent. A coach who may be facing a more talented opponent, a wiser and more experienced coach, a more experienced team, or other circumstances that he can do nothing about still must try to use tactics that will give his or her team a chance to win.

The Importance of Conditioning

One factor exists that the coach can do something about—the physical condition of his or her team. While a coach may have to accept certain factors, one aspect a coach should never accept is to allow his or her team to be beaten because the other coach outworked him. Superior conditioning can allow a less-talented team to beat more-talented personnel. When players get tired, mistakes occur. Transition will become slower and less intense, the quickness in picking up the ball lessens, and communication and adjustment to defensive responsibilities tend to become slack. This scenario usually happens in the latter stages of a game, which are usually the most important stages. If a coach has this advantage, his or her team should make full use of it.

A tendency exists for coaches to believe that conditioning applies principally to offense—getting out on the break, running the lane, ball and player movement in the offensive sets, etc. In reality, however, conditioning pertains mainly to defense. Another adage of the game is that "if rest is needed, do it on offense when you have the ball, never on defense when the opponent has the ball." Obviously, when a team has the ball, it can't get hurt if it decides to slow down the tempo. Because team defense is a five-player operation, one slow-reacting player can break down the defense. Accordingly, a team should never let up or rest defensively.

Successful defense involves many components. None is more important than conditioning. It is hard to imagine an effective, successful defensive team that is not well conditioned. Conditioning a basketball team is hard work for both the coaches and the players. There are no easy paths to becoming a well-conditioned team. Proper conditioning places a physical demand on the players that taxes their stamina and energy. During the time devoted to conditioning, the physical challenges the coach requires from the players should exceed the demands of the day before. Each day this demand should increase during the period devoted to this essential aspect of the team's development.

The coach should always realize that these repetitive physical demands are made in order to enable the team to play the last minutes of a game as effectively as the first minutes of the game. Almost any team can play the first minutes of a game without too much concern for physical preparation. To be able to run the court offensively and defensively, to maintain defensive pressure on and off the ball, to fill an outside lane in a fast break, and to retreat at full speed to the line of the ball on transition defense are a few examples of the numerous benefits superior conditioning affords a team in the latter minutes of a game. Furthermore, an opponent that is not well-conditioned will play less effectively off the ball, take short cuts in transition, and rely on teammates to pick up an opponent because he or she is too tired to retreat on defense at full speed. Offensively, less effective screens, more offensive standing around, and less team movement are other symptoms of poorly-conditioned teams. Furthermore, tired legs result in poor shooting from the floor.

The three important phases of team organization from the first practice to the first official game are conditioning, organization, and refinement—in that order. A coach should never allow the program to minimize the importance of conditioning. Few coaches are able to effectively condition a team after the schedule of games commences. The sore muscles, the heavy legs, the shortness of stamina and the lack of endurance can be tolerated before the actual schedule begins. If a team and its players experience such conditions after the first third or more of the schedule, they will suffer negative consequences—psychologically, as well as performance-wise. A team maintains its conditioning in this period and during the season, but builds the strong muscles, develops their legs and in creases the level of stamina in its early pre-schedule practices. Accordingly, coaches should give real attention to their daily, weekly and monthly practice plans that embrace conditioning, organization of offense and defense, and the refinement of these factors.

The special situations a team is confronted with—out of bounds play, jump ball line-ups, proper use of the clock and other elements of play—are all part of the third phase. Conditioning, while principally achieved in the first part of the program schedule, should always be given thought and time throughout the entire schedule. Simply, a coach doesn't initially condition his or her team and then conclude "that's done" and go away from it for the rest of the season. A coach should always be aware of slippage. It can happen to teams that begin well conditioned. Lack of time and attention to this factor can cause slippage. Without superior conditioning, a press defense has little chance to be really effective and consistent in its play.

Defensive Rules of Pressure Defenses

The impact of the physical abilities and weaknesses of a team's personnel should be recognized as they affect its ability to effective play pressure defenses, including:

- The greater a team's speed and quickness, the more a pressure defense can be extended over the entire court surface.
- It is important to try to determine as quickly as possible the opponent's strategy and plan to combat your press.
- The coach should devise a counter to the opponent's plan without giving up easy baskets.
- Being able to counter the initial offensive plan of the opponent and being able to subtly counter it with a countering deployment are important.
- The coach should understand that while the opponent will usually have offensive tendencies that are constant each game and will exhibit similar consistencies for their type of offense against the press, an opponent's counter to a team's pressure is usually unknown.
- The press defense initially employed is a probing defense—not intended to steal or force turnovers but to determine the opponent's tactics to attack and beat the press.
- If the counter is too complicated to communicate in a time-out, the coach should wait until half-time and make the adjustments needed.
- The coach should emphasize that team defense is a five-player defense, and that each player must always stay within the team-defensive framework.
- Although a press defense is not the surprise defense it once was, like the various changing zone defenses, it must be read and recognized as to its weaknesses.
- To employ a press defense effectively over the course of a season, players should learn the counters necessary to keep it effective and how to read and react to the opponent's change. A press can be especially effective in tournament play.

Strenths of the Press Defense

No other phase of basketball has created as many theories of use as has the press defense. It incorporates the strengths and often the alignment of the basic team half-court defenses—the assigned-individual defense. By incorporating the zone defenses and ball pressure the switch defense can cause considerable concern for an opponent. Among the many ways that a press defense can help a team are the following:

- It can establish a quicker tempo of offensive play for an up-tempo team.

- It can create turnovers, e.g., interceptions, charge fouls on the opponent, careless ball handling, loose balls, violations, etc.

- It can make conditioning a real factor in the game's outcome by the ball pressure and the quicker tempo it can create.

- It can cause an opponent to devote more game preparation time to solving the opponent's press and to underprepare the offense for the game.

- It can be a surprise element that can cause adjustment problems for an offense that is not prepared for such a defense.

- The press has an amoeba quality that has become more and more popular. It takes on different forms—the full court, the half court, and the three-quarter court. It can involve several different alignments, such as the 1-3-1 zone type, 1-2-2, 1-2-1-1, etc. To compound the offensive team's problems, a 1-3-1 can change to a 1-2-1-1, or vice versa, and a 1-2-2 can easily change to a 2-2-1. Each zone alignment, similar to the situation in attacking the half-court zones, demands that the offensive team be able to recognize the passing lanes and attack each particular zone press at its weaknesses. This feature illustrates the "amoeba" nature of the press defense. Similar to the zone alignment, a team initially attacks the changes with which it is confronted. The changes thus create a new offensive recognition, different passing lanes and different personnel deployment. As a result, with a 10-second time element thrown into the mix, the offense can have serious problems determining its attack.

- It can allow a team well behind in points to get back into the game and possibly win if the opponent is not prepared for a gambling-type press.

- It can cause real problems to a team with slow players.

- It can expose lack of preparation in teams.

- It can be an important weapon for a team in a championship game or in a game that has much greater pressure than normal. One of the most common mistakes a coach may make in these high-pressure games is to inadvertently prepare negatively: "Don't do this; don't do that," etc. The possible result will be a team on its heels, not wanting to make a mistake. In other words, a team that is playing too carefully. I have found that the aggressive, committed, and competitive attitude a press defense can give a team will enable it to begin the game in a positive frame of mind. The annual Super Bowl is an example of this negative preparation. The extra week of practice allotted to Super Bowl teams subsequently becomes a week of negativeness. More film study, more planning, and more preparation cause some teams to over prepare, and they never really get out of the blocks. Over the years, Super Bowl games have not always been the exciting and competitive games the public expects. During one recent year, the Super Bowl teams had only their normal one-week period to prepare. Well played and exciting, the game resembled the games the fans had seen all year.

The point to be remembered is that because an important game in itself can cause players to be overcautious, a coach can combat this attitude by employing a press defense that literally can "recharge" the players' minds towards the immediate need for intensity, all-out effort, high degree focus, etc.

Given its numerous benefits, it can only be surmised that the press defense is a weapon every team should possess. The type of press, its use, and the experience of a team are factors the coach must take into account when adding the press to a team's defensive arsenal.

Weaknesses of the Press Defense

As in any defense, certain inherent weaknesses exist, including the following in the press defense:

- A press defensive team can never be certain of the game plan the opponent has chosen to counteract the press. The half-court offense will vary little from game to game, but the press offense can involve many varieties.

- The amount of court area the press must cover creates problems. For example, some coaches feel the full-court press is beyond the quickness and endurance of the press defense team. Retreating to a 3/4 or 1/2 court press narrows the defensive area so that a full court does not have to be used.

- An inexperienced team will initially have problems with the physical and mental demands of the press.

- The quicker the team, the more extended its press can be. Accordingly, slower teams should be half-court press teams in most instances. A slow team should not be over extended if a coach wants to employ a successful press.

- A press defense normally can only get better with experience. A coach should remember that initially playing a press defense is a learning experience that should involve the players learning from their earlier mistakes. A danger in playing the press is presumption. The coach should beware of presuming that the opponent is going to react only one way and thus preparing the team only for this anticipated reaction.

- The coach should be prepared to abandon the press and go to the normal half-court defense if the opponent has a plan to counter the press for which the pressing team is not prepared. However, the team should try to stay in the press long enough to determine the offensive team's spacing, player alignment, and the type attack.

- One weak defender can render a press ineffective and be even more damaging than a breakdown in the normal half-court defense. In the normal half-court defense, the defense can ordinarily rotate and lessen the damage, but in a press, the defenders are not positioned to rotate effectively. This can result in unopposed lay-ups for the opponent.

Summary-the Press Defense

Many evaluations should be made by the coach before the type of defensive press is chosen which best suits a team's personnel and their abilities. The bench strength, particularly as it applies to numbers, is another element to weigh. From a strategic standpoint, it would be wise to try to determine the opponent's offensive plan of attack without getting blown out early in the game. A conservative press with bark but no bite can be of help in this instance. Simply, if a team can give the appearance of its regular press without the aggressiveness it normally displays, the opponent's plan can be unveiled, and the team hasn't given up anything. When the pressing coach has confidence that the opponent's plan is known and the press can counter the offensive plan of the opponent, then the aggressive normal press can be employed with whatever adjustment or counters the pressing coach feels are appropriate. As such, there is a cat-and-mouse scenario when playing a press.

CHAPTER 10

OTHER DEFENSIVE TOPICS

NEW PROPOSED RULES

No Foul-Out Rule

As the game of basketball has grown nationally and internationally, the outcome of games often seem to be determined less by the players and more often by the referees. The game has gone from a rule book that looked like a small pamphlet to a small-sized book containing rules and interpretations that resembles a phone directory of a small city. While the importance of basketball's rules committees' staying abreast of the game's changes, the question must be addressed: "in the process, are we being *over* ruled?" It is my contention that the role of the officials in determining the game's outcome should be reduced—not expanded. Basketball referees will always be needed, but how much? Many of the game's top officials agree with the principle I propose.

The main purpose of a no foul-out rule would be to lessen the effect one call can have on a game. Sometimes, a questionable call will occur, as the game tape will show, yet its impact on the game's outcome may be decisive. It doesn't have to be the call at the end of the game. Rather, some of the calls that most affect a game's outcome are early fouls on a key player that result in an early substitution for this key player with too many early fouls. While the coach of this player doesn't have to substitute for him with many minutes still left in the half, if he or she doesn't and this key player has but one foul left and there is still much of the game to be played, the coach will be subject to undue criticism from the media, spectators, and probably the athletic director or general manager for whom he or she is working. This key player may be the most important part of the team's game plan. Accordingly, the early loss of this player's court presence will often prove to be the main reason the game was lost. Whether they were legitimate fouls or ticky-tack calls, the loss of this player on the court seriously impairs the team's chances of winning.

In this regard, a problem that is frequently referred to today that has existed in the past and probably will always be a problem concerns home-court advantage. Part of the advantage that home teams are perceived to have over visiting teams can be the reluctance of officials to foul out the star player of the home team. This factor is particularly true in the NBA. Wilt Chamberlain never fouled out of a game in his entire NBA career, and when was the last time Michael Jordan fouled out before his retirement? It puts a real pressure on an official to call an eliminating foul on the home team's star, and it's a source of pressure with which the official shouldn't have to deal.

With the no foul-out rule, the decision would lie with the coach whether he wants to keep this player in the game and risk the severity of the fifth foul (college and high school rule) or the sixth (NBA rule). In the NBA, it is even more difficult to hide a player defensively because of the "no zone" rule. Most coaches and many officials with whom I have discussed this proposal concur. Coaches (and many officials) would prefer it to be a coach's decision whether a particular player remains in the game. Although historically, the best officials have kept the game under control, no one wants the officials to be in a situation where they have to decide who the winning team is.

What makes this foul-out rule so sacrosanct? The fact that we started with four fouls, then five, and now it's six at the NBA level is an indication that something is wrong. Will the foul-out rule go to seven before long? Then eight? The past history would indicate this might be the case. Or should the no foul-out rule be adopted and make a big step in returning the play of the game to the players and their coaches?

The only possibly coherent reason I have heard to question the proposed change in the foul-out rule is that the game could get out of control. Rules already exist in the rule book today that prevent a coach or a player from making mockery of the rule by obvious, intentional fouls. These could be strengthened at all levels of play. A prior warning by the head official should be given to the player and coach that obvious, intentional fouls will not be tolerated. Also, the scorer's bench must be made aware of the warning. If the player persists in his or her fouling intentionally, it would be cause for expulsion of both player and coach. Furthermore, a letter of condemnation would be sent to the president, chancellor or principal of the school advising that particular controlling authority of the infraction. A fine could be the result. At the NBA level, it would be much simpler—a sizeable fine for both the player and the coach. If the coach is aware of the travesty of the game his or her player is causing and the fine to which the coach will be subjected, chances are relatively slim that the coach will not remove the player from the game. At both collegiate and high school level, the coach's athletic director should also receive a copy of the letter of reprimand.

The purpose of the proposed rule is to reduce the effect of a referee on a game's outcome and to give the coach an appropriate level of the authority and impact on the outcome of the game. A player committing a flagrant foul and receiving a technical foul that causes expulsion is a situation that doesn't pertain to this rule. Those rules are in the book and should always be kept there.

If my proposed rule change were to be adopted, there will be no limit on the number of fouls a player may receive in the course of a game. However, the five-foul limit for high school and college programs will be kept in place. At the NBA level, the six-foul limit will likewise be kept. In the event a player exceeds the foul limit, any subsequent foul by this player will be a two-shot foul and will result in the retaining of ball possession by the fouled player and fouled team. The decision will rest with the coach whether to bench the player who has exceeded the foul limit. There will be no automatic expulsion rule for excessive fouls. The proposed rule in no way infringes on the present rules of expulsion, since they refer to excessive technical fouls, fighting or abuse.

The Time-Clock Rule

A certain degree of caution and awareness must come into play concerning the limit of the shot clock. Differences exist in the time-clock limit at the three different levels of play—college, the NBA, and the international game. For example, colleges have relatively less-experienced players and limits on their practice time; the NBA has its no-zone rule and shortness of its time clock; and the international game has the international and FIBA rules, the international court markings and the vast-reaching perimeters of the game that is played on the international level. Each of these differences between competitive levels has implications that must be considered when establishing an appropriate time-clock rule for a particular level of competition.

The worth of the 24-second clock of the NBA is debatable. Have the coaches caught up with it and changed their game tactics enough to cause a rethinking of its time clock? The fact that the excitement of the NBA has lessened appreciably this past decade, that the scoring has annually dwindled, and that the fast-paced game that brought the NBA into its original prominence has slowed are reasons to question the "why" of these changes. To point to an individual such as Michael Jordan and the great impact he had on the game as testimony that the game has not suffered in its excitement is avoiding the facts. As great as Michael Jordan's impact on the game of basketball has been, he is not greater than the game itself.

Simply, NBA coaches have caught up with the 24-second clock as it is now interpreted. As has been pointed out in this book, the perimeter-spaced offense that counters the double-down post defense and permits the transition of the offense to defense can defend the opponent's fast break or transition offense without problem. The result is the walk-up type offense with very few fast-break opportunities after either the made field goal or the missed field goal by the opponent. The three-point shot has been fingered as the culprit. It is not the culprit. Blame lies with the shortness of the time clock. If the perimeter offensive player has but five or six seconds left on the time clock, the perimeter player who has received the outlet pass from the double-down post player has only a few options. Coaches are mentally trained to make rules work for them. As a point of fact, they have defensively caught up with the 24-second clock in its present form. If the clock began when the ball passed midcourt, it would seriously affect the positive use of the double-down defense, as well as increase the number of options for the perimeter offensive player. Instead of five or six seconds of clock time left, twelve to fourteen seconds would be the case. It would create a moving half-court offense, instead of the present stand-around perimeter offense so common today in the NBA.

The 35-second college clock has seemed to keep the college game in balance. The numerous types of defenses played today at the college and high school levels demand more time for the offense to read and adjust to these many defenses. I'm not convinced it should be shortened. College basketball has never before had the media and public acceptance it now enjoys. The NCAA post-season tournament (particularly the Final Four) is vivid testimony to the fact that collegiate basketball's annual exercise to determine a champion rivals the World Series of baseball and NFL's Super Bowl in both interest and acceptance.

Internationally, the 30-second clock seems to be popularly accepted worldwide. In fact, many individuals believe the NBA should adopt the 30-second clock. When the international game of 40 minutes, the number of points scored, and the pace of the international game are examined and the reduction in number of points in the 48-minute NBA game and the NBA's game pace are considered, it begs a re-examination of the time clocks of each game—the FIBA game and the NBA. It should be noted that the FIBA game permits the zone defense, whereas the NBA has a "no-zone" rule. With the present 24-second clock, it is appropriate to have the "no zone" rule. On the other hand, if the clock time were to be expanded, the NBA could possibly play the same game as does the rest of the world. Only in the NBA is one of the more common defenses in all basketball—the zone and its variations—excluded.

Raising the Basket

In the 1960s, a popular national magazine of the time, *Look* magazine, wanted to have an experiment on the worth of the 12-foot basket. The "dunk" was gaining in popularity, and the purists of the game opposed the tactic. They felt the basket was too low and that the game was being taken over by the dunk maneuver. Because of the composition and size of the ball prior to World War II, no one really dunked a ball. The lack of pebbling on the ball's surface and the ball being slightly larger than today's ball, especially the NBA-sized ball, meant that the dunk was rare. Furthermore, few floors had any spring to them; players didn't jump nearly as high as today's players. This situation gave even more reasons to those opposing the dunk.

After the war, the athleticism level of basketball became greater, ball size and surface became standard, and court surfaces improved—all factors contributing to the popularity of the dunk. The purists were worried. The skills for playing basketball would diminish, and the dunk would take over. In a sense, they were correct since many players who play above the rim today have never developed an ambidexterity in the basket area shooting a basketball. Furthermore, a 10-12 foot shot is practiced only slightly by these high-jumping inside players. In a sense, the dunk proves to be fool's gold since the higher the competitive level of play, the less the dunk is effective, especially in a half-court game. Tim Cohane, one of sport's greatest writers and the sports editor of *Look* magazine, asked me to conduct an experiment of a 12-foot basket and the type game it would provide. With the permission of the NCAA, Cal was allowed to experiment with the concept. We had four days of practice to adjust to the raised 12-foot basket. None of us really knew what kind of game it would bring about. Although the results were interesting, no conclusion could be reached based on only one game and four practices. We had two players who were 7-feet tall and could block shots, and we had players who were schooled principally in the half-court game.

Statistics were kept that were surprising in some areas. There were no dunks. We had no blocked shots. Players who played a system of play that produced 65 or slightly more shots a game found themselves in a transition, fast-break game that produced about 90 shots per team. Foul-shooting percentages were in the 40s, and field-goal percentages in the mid- to upper-20s. A lay-up was the most difficult shot, because it wasn't a normal-type lay-up but a real floor-type shot. Most shots were taken from the perimeter (one player practiced the old two-handed set shot), and the rebound from a missed shot was a long rebound in the vicinity of the foul-circle area. This scenario encouraged the transition, fast-break type game. The height of the basket caused the trajectory of the floor shot to be raised to a point where the resulting angle change kept it from being blocked. In fairness to the shooting percentages, they would undoubtedly rise if enough practice were afforded the players.

Prior to this experiment, I was, frankly, on the fence regarding the raised basket. Most coaches were against it. The experiment, however, showed some of their arguments (e.g. a slow-paced game, etc.), to be invalid. On the other hand, it did prove to me that 12 feet is too high, as it could rob basketball of the most exciting part of the game—the fast break and the ensuing lay-up. Probably in time, change may prevail, but baseball has survived well with its 90-foot bases and 60-foot plus pitching distance. Frankly, I would try other methods to rectify what many would consider an imbalance in the game. If the feeling persists and gains support, I would caution the rules committee to experiment extensively before any adoption.

Summary—New Proposed Rules

Coaches must never lose sight of the need for change that basketball has demanded over its many years. The impact of the change on the game should be fully examined. As such, the self-interest of individuals or groups should never be allowed to dictate change. Before a major rules change is adopted nationally, experimentation by a conference or conferences must be done in order to evaluate thoroughly the strengths and weaknesses fo the change. To take the view that the game is great as is and adopt the questionable adage of "If it's not broken, don't fix it" could have us still playing the old center-jump game. In a sense, the NBA's philosophy has been "Don't change". As a result, the NBA's game has been permitted to deteriorate in its excitement and pace. Even the motor of an automobile that is running needs periodic oil changes and engine adjustments to keep it running satisfactorily. Such is true of the game of basketball if imbalances are to be foreseen, identified, and corrected.

THE BEST DEFENSIVE PLAYERS

In the many decades I have been associated with the game of basketball, I thought it would be fitting to list the players at their best positions defensively and the teams I have seen in both college and NBA who struck me as the best I have seen. It is always an arguable tack to pick the best of anything, but these are players and teams I have either coached against or have personally seen play.

Centers

Bill Russell

Bill is the single most dominant defender, I believe, that the game has ever seen. To fully appreciate his impact on the game was to have had to face his team on the court. The record of his teams' successes, both in college and the NBA, is beyond what any other individual has accomplished. With the University of San Francisco, he led the Dons to two NCAA championships, and a record total of consecutive wins that reached into the sixties (UCLA's great teams in the eighties topped this record). His nine NBA championships in ten years is further evidence of his impact. His remarkably quick leap, his flexed-knee stance that allowed him to take a pump fake without changing his stance and his ability to raise shot blocking to an art form were exceptional. Many fast breaks were the result of his directing the block toward his perimeter defenders who then initiated the fast break. Coach Red Auerbach built his great Celtic teams around this remarkable talent, and the game history is evidence of Red's wisdom.

Wilt Chamberlain

Wilt was a great athlete and a force at both ends of the court. Records didn't reflect shot blocks other than single post-game reporting. No official stats were kept, so it's not possible to actually know his seasonal averages. He was easily the best shot blocker of his time other than Bill Russell. Wilt had great speed in his earlier years and ran the court well. He played more 48-minute games than any player in the history of the NBA.

Bill Walton

During his college career and for the early years of his NBA career, Bill enjoyed good health. However, a persistent foot injury created many problems in the latter years of his NBA career. At UCLA, he was the dominant shot blocker and defensive center in college basketball. The Bruins won three NCAA championships, and while with the Portland Trail Blazers, he helped bring coach Jack Ramsey and his team to their first and only NCAA championship. His mechanics of defensive rebounding were fundamentally sound and allowed him to be an outstanding outlet passer for the initiation of the fast break.

Strong or Power Forwards

Dennis Rodman

Dennis was probably the most versatile defender in the history of the game. Throughout his career in the NBA, Rodman was called upon to defend point guards, #2 guards, small forwards, power forwards and occasionally centers. At every defensive position, he managed to do better than his team's normal defender at those positions. He used his extremely quick feet and hands, great physical effort, an intuitive sense for defending, and a wiry strength to successfully defend players who were much taller, heavier, and stronger. Another defensive strength was his mobility and agility in denying his opponent the ball when defending the post-up opponent. In spite of being one of the smaller power forwards, he was the leading rebounder for the majority of his years in the NBA. While in college, he averaged a rebound in less than every two minutes his senior year. At every competitive level, he was a remarkable defender.

Karl Malone

Karl's defensive game doesn't have outstanding statistics in any particular area except that he plays both ends of the court every night in every game in spite of injury and pain. The best accolade a basketball player can be given is that "he is a lunch-pail player." He comes to compete, will physically challenge an opponent, and makes the transition from offense to defense without hesitation and at full speed. He can play size because of his strength, quickness, and intelligence. He will probably go down as the all-around greatest power forward the game has seen. His record of continuous play will be as a benchmark in basketball for all future players, as Cal Ripken's is in baseball.

Small Forwards

Scotty Pippen

Scotty is another versatile defender who can defend two offensive positions, the small forward and the #2 guard. His quickness creates real problems for his opponents as he denies wing entries as few other small forwards have done. When defending the ball, his quickness and reactions, along with his quick hands, can make an opponent miserable. He has the mental requirements needed for an outstanding defender—initiating, anticipation, resourcefulness, and determination to shut off his opponent. These same mental requirements, along with his physical qualities, enable him to guard the quickness and the speed of many #2 guards. His alertness on transition from offense to defense creates many interceptions in this phase of the game. He has been a constant starter on the "All Defensive NBA" teams.

Michael Cooper

Because Michael came off the bench, he was never given the acclaim in basketball that he should have received. Small forwards dreaded his defending against them. He was extremely quick with long arms, and he accepted his role of being a defensive stopper. No one denied a wing player better. His quickness and agility made it difficult to beat him one-on-one. He was very aggressive and alert on defending the post #1 player and was very strong. No one could ever intimidate him, and he would never back down. He jumped well and could block shots inside. He loved the challenge that defense can give a player. The better the player, the more he accepted the challenge. He could defend a point, a #2 and a small forward. It doesn't get much better than that.

Jim Pollard

Jim was a mainstay, along with George Mikan, a Hall-of-Fame center, for the Minneapolis Lakers. They were the perennial champions of the NBA in the fifties, prior to moving to Los Angeles. Jim was a 6'5", lanky player who was considered the best all-around NBA player of his time. He was extremely quick and learned defensive fundamentals when he played on Coach Everett Dean's Stanford NCAA championship team in 1941. He could deny the wing opponent, defend the post-up player and had a great sense of anticipation that enabled him to steal many passes. Ahead of the game defensively during his time, he could be an outstanding defender today, as well as being one of the game's top offensive players. He is another Hall of Famer, and his defense was no small part of this recognition.

#2 Guards

Michael Jordan

It is interesting that many of the game's great offensive players were great defenders. What made Michael the great defender he was? I believe because he embodied every basic fundamental that is associated with great defense. Physically, he was cat-quick; he used his feet as well as his hands; and was seldom in a poorly-balanced position. Mentally, he was alert, used fakes to set up his opponent and initiated action, not waiting to be faked. Often, his initiative caused his offensive opponent to be defensive in order to stave off a steal. When he moved up his defensive intensity, he seemed to ignite his teammates, making the Chicago Bulls close to impossible for an opponent to run their normal offense against. His annual steal statistics were testimony to this great player's total commitment to winning.

Oscar Robertson

Again, in addition to being one of our greatest offensive players in the history of the game, Oscar was also an exceptional defender. It makes me a real believer that to ever reach the heights of an Oscar, Michael and a Jerry West, pride is a common attribute. These men were great offensive players in every phase—scoring, passing, dribbling, and working on their total game, and it included defense. I had the privilege of coaching Oscar in the 1960 Olympics, and I marveled at his great understanding of defense both on and off the ball. His fundamentals—stance, footwork, and use of hands—were textbook, and he was as competitive as any defender you would see. He had the size to defend inside as well as the perimeter; nothing fancy—just fundamentally solid.

Hank Luisetti

Hank was one of the real greats of the early game. While he revolutionized the game offensively (he introduced the one-handed set shot to the game in the 30's), he was also a great defensive player. His great intuitive sense of defense caused him to be as much a problem defensively as he was offensively. He was very quick, had outstanding court speed, and had the same sixth sense that all the great defenders seem to possess. He was one of the West's best high jumpers during his Stanford collegiate career, which caused him to leap far beyond his actual height, which was 6'3". His ability to turn an interception into a transition basket gave him a dimensional play few other players had. He could, and would, be an outstanding player today, as his skill level was far above any player in the country. As a player he scored 50 points against a highly-ranked Duquesne team of the time. Scoring fifty points was an unbelievable achievement at the time, since many teams averaged but forty points, or slightly more, a game. He followed this performance on his Stanford scoring tour of the East, with 28 points in leading his team to an upset win against an undefeated Long Island team considered by many as the nation's best. Both games were road games that were lopsided wins that introduced the basketball world to Hank Luisetti.

Point Guards

K.C. Jones

Few players were as adept at playing the ball from baseline to baseline as K.C. Jones. He was very strong for a point and stood 6'2". He possessed very quick feet and even quicker hands. Like Bill Russell, K.C. played an important part on the greatest defensive squad and most dominant defensive team in the history of the NBA. The press defense was their staple, and K.C. was at his best defending a dribbler in the open court. However, he was also an effective half-court defender and always drew the opponent that needed shutting down. He played Tom Gola—one of the finest players in the history of Eastern college basketball—and shut him down. Tom was the leader who took LaSalle to the final NCAA game in 1956. K.C. gave away more than seven inches and showed his versatility as a defender. Like Russell, his accomplishments are best reflected in his two NCAA championships and nine NBA rings.

Jerry West

When I watched Jerry West play, I saw the same intelligence, the great anticipatory sense, the quickness of movement, and the exceptional reflexes that I had seen years before in Hank Luisetti. Jerry studied the opponent's offense and was able to intercept or deflect the inside passer from a position off the ball. He was probably as good an off-the-ball defender as I've ever seen. His physical gifts and deep competitiveness made many opponents worry about the off-the-ball problems he caused. Jerry was blessed with great foot speed and quick hands and took the one-on-one defensive situation as competitively as he did his offense. His ability to turn over an opponent's errant pass or fumbled ball to a quick transition basket was another positive relating to his defensive game. He was another member of my 1960 Rome Olympic team. As a result, I had the up-close opportunity to appreciate his greatness at both ends of the court.

Walt Frazier

Walt was a key component defensively of one of the best balanced teams in NBA history—the New York Knicks of the early 70's. Walt was the leading ball stealer in the league and turned many games around when the Knicks needed a turnaround. He was lightning quick with his hands. Although he did not possess Michael Jordan's and Jerry West's foot speed, he was a real problem nonetheless for his opponents. Accordingly, every coach in the NBA tried to minimize his defensive impact on the game's outcome. Because he had one of the most intelligent teams behind him, he was free to gamble on defense. Gamble he did, and he was usually the winner. Probably no other team rotated with the understanding and quickness of the Knicks. As I have stated, the intelligence factor was a major contribution to their success and in their allowing Walt to become the feared defender of that period.

Summary—the Best Defensive Players

Picking All-Star teams and players will always be a highly subjective and personal task. I'm sure there are defenders that many might rate over these players. I selected players that I either coached at one time or saw many times. As I pointed out, it is remarkable the number of instances in which these players were as outstanding offensively as they were defensively. This observation only serves to reinforce the fact that the pride of being the best offensively often spills over into great defense, resulting in exceptionally complete players.

THE BEST DEFENSIVE TEAMS

I find the defensive prowess of a team to be the major factor in reaching the level of championship play. Football annually emphasizes this fact, especially in the NFL. It's hard for me to remember an average or above-average college defensive team winning an NCAA championship. From the middle '50s to the '80s and beyond, the NCAA winners were highly regarded defensive teams. The following list presents the NBA teams and the college teams that I feel were the best defensive teams I have seen over the years. Because of the dramatic changes in the rules just prior to World War II, I can relate only to these post-War teams.

NBA Teams

Boston Celtics

The Bill Russell and K.C. Jones years of the Celtics were the most dominant teams the league had ever seen. Their many championships are irrefutable indications that they were the greatest. No one player ever dominated the game as Russell did during these years. His shot blocking ability has never been challenged and even more formidable was the intimidation Russell created for an opponent. This was the first full-court press team to play effectively over the full course of the game. Red Auerbach, their legendary coach, had never coached this type of basketball, and few college teams in the Midwest and East employed the press as their basic defense. I believe this was another indication of why Red Auerbach is regarded as the greatest NBA coach of all time. Coaches should learn from Red's flexibility of thought. He drafted K.C. Jones and traded for Bill Russell and changed his offensive and defensive concepts to fit his personnel. Too many coaches try to fit star players into a system that reduces the impact that the star player can have on a team.

Chicago Bulls

The dominant team of the 1990's, the Bulls team was one that seemed to get better with age. When the basic personnel of these great Bulls teams is analyzed, the fact is striking that the team had three of the finest individual defenders—Jordan, Pippin and Rodman—who have ever played the game. In its makeup, the Bulls of the late 1990's didn't resemble the Celtics. As an unbelievable player in the middle, Russell was the team's main man with great defenders around him—the defensive core of the successful Celtics. The Bulls did not have a dominant man in the middle. Their real strength was their ability to change the tempo of the defense as a unit and create totally different problems for the offense. The conversion rate on the turnovers that aggressive defensive change brings to an opponent is difficult to adjust to for any team. The Bull's ability to run off 15-to-2 type scoring runs as a result of this change took opponents out of many games. The infusion of Rodman with his numerous defensive gifts, especially on the defensive backboard, gave them a dimension they previously did not enjoy. Unfortunately, this team has been broken up as their contracts ran out. Wile some consider the Bulls the equal of the Celtics, the tremendous influence of Bill Russell convinces me that there has never been a better defensive team than the Celtics, especially once Satch Sanders became a regular. Bull's Coach Phil Jackson hired two of the best defensive minds in basketball—John Bach and Jimmy Rogers—to put Chicago's juggernaut together, and the three coaches did an outstanding job.

New York Knicks

I loved watching this team play in the late '60s, and early '70s. Beautifully coached by Red Holzman, they were the forerunners of the defense that is played today. The defense of today to which I refer is the offensive spacing that enables the two wings and the guards to make an immediate transition from an outside shot. As a result, scores continue to drop, fast-break basketball is disappearing slowly but surely except for the loose-ball recovery or an interception, and very little offensive rebounding occurs except by the post player. The Knicks would employ similar tactics when they played a high-scoring, running-type team by having center Willis Reed rebound, and Bill Bradley and Dave DeBusschere ignore the offensive board and return quickly on their transition defense. As a result, they were the most difficult team to play in the league, especially if the opponent needed a fast-tempo game. Much to my dismay, no one followed Coach Holzman's tactics, which made their defense even more effective.

The Knicks relied on their half-court defense, which they felt was the best in the league. Their record pretty well substantiates their thinking. As I related earlier, they were led by the defensive initiative and opportunism of Walt Frazier and rotated as a unit as well as a team could. Though they were not blessed with a lot of foot speed individually, their communication and vision more than made up for it. It was a very intelligent basketball team—DeBusschere, Bradley, Reed, Frazier and Earl Monroe—with an experienced coach who had league-wide respect for his being innovative and creative—Red Holzman.

College Teams

Because the college and NBA games are distinctly different due to the differences in the rules, I am listing the three best collegiate defensive programs I have seen in my time.

USF—(1954-1956)

The great USF defensive teams occurred during the Bill Russell and K.C. Jones era. USF was an effective full-court press team that learned to funnel the ball in to their dominator—Bill Russell. As the years went by, Russell became very adept not only at shot blocking, but also at directing the block to K.C. Jones, with a fast-break basket the usual result.

Because shot blocking was not emphasized, opponents were not prepared for the block. I coached the West team in the Hearst Fresh Air Fund game at Madison Square Garden in 1956. It was the premier All-Star Senior post-season game, and every college player dreamed of participating. Fortunately, I had Bill Russell and K.C. Jones on my team. The East team had many name players—most notably Tommy Heinsohn, the ex-player and later coach of the Celtics. The East players had never seen Russell. I have never seen players so openly dismayed by the ability of Bill Russell to block any shot within 16 to 18 feet of the basket—and once from over 20 feet. The game turned into a rout as Russell would block the shot to K.C., and K.C. would end up laying the ball in for two points. One

East player had his first three shots blocked and refused to shoot after that. Bill and K.C. anchored the most effective defensive collegiate team I've ever seen.

UCLA—(1964-1975)

Johnny Wooden's 1964 NCAA champion team was his first really effective press defensive team. It was an unusual team—Fred Slaughter, his center, was 6'5". The team played a 1-2-1-1 defense with the center, Slaughter, picking up the passer at the baseline. No aggressive denial was performed by the two front-zone defenders. However, after the pass in from out of bounds, Slaughter and the defender in the zone where the opponent seized the ball doubled the player with the ball, but not too aggressively. Although it was not an aggressive press, it didn't allow easy baskets as the safety man, Keith Erickson, was a tremendous athlete and was seldom caught out of position. UCLA's original 1-2-1-1 was their basic starting zone press that they used to determine the opponent's plan of attack. When the opponent's approach to handle UCLA's press was subsequently identified, Coach Wooden and his staff would adjust to counter the opponent's plan. It could become either a 1-3-1 or a 2-2-1. This tactic is called a complementing press, and it can be very effective. UCLA teams under Coach Wooden executed this complementary change better than any press team I ever observed. My Michigan State, Cal and USF teams used other theories of press defenses. While we were good at making the change, the UCLA teams were the best. The change they employed was able effectively to counter the opponents, and few opponents could counter UCLA's counter. It was an important part of their great success. To demonstrate the versatility a press defense can give a team, both USF and UCLA were extremely successful programs—but their theories of the press differed dramatically.

UNLV

Although UNLV was not a press team, the Rebels' 1989-90 team was the toughest half-court defensive team I ever saw at the college level. What made it so difficult for an opponent was the 5-second rule interpretation at the time. It was a strict individual-type defense with the defender on the ball widely stanced, low-based with his knees flexed, and tight on the ball. Guy Anthony was usually on the opponent's point player. The wing players were tightly played in a denial stance. The post player fronted and played on the ballside high, while the fifth defender also denied. The wide stance was practiced daily by Coach Jerry Tarkanian. This inside lateral stance made it difficult for the ball handler to penetrate as this UNLV team was composed of five quick, active athletes who took great pride in their defense. The pressure of the 5-second count brought about many bad passes, stolen dribbles, and other turnovers. It was a half-court defense that seldom played as a press defense. The ball pressure exerted on the ball handler was sound fundamentally—movement of feet, low stance, and very good lateral movement. Although relatively simple in appearance, UNLV's defensive execution was difficult to play against and a beauty to see as an observer. Coach Tarkanian practiced his team's defense on the ball daily, and it showed in his team's execution.

It is important to note that the three outstanding college teams that best impressed me were distinctly different in their play. I have also been favorably impressed by other programs that exhibited great defensive principles of play, notably the Indiana teams of the 80's and before that the teams Coach Henry Iba annually produced at Oklahoma State in the '40s and the '50s.

If I may be permitted a boast, a team that enjoyed a reputation of playing exceptional defense in the late '50s were my Cal teams. We led the country in both the 1958-59 and 1959-60 seasons and won 44 out of 45 games during this period. We were comparable to the New York Knicks—not greatly gifted physically but smart and fundamentally sound with a fine shot blocker, Darryl Imhoff. We played the press with the complementary feature of the UCLA teams who came several years later in the '60s, and we prided ourselves on our half-court defense. I would like to say we were as effective as UNLV, but no team I've seen played the half-court defense as well as the 1990 UNLV NCAA championship team.

Summary—the Best Defensive Teams

I believe that all the teams that I have selected as those that have most impressed me defensively showed a deep commitment to defense, an intelligent understanding of the team aspects of defense, and an unselfish approach to doing whatever is necessary win. It is also interesting to note that all these highly-rated defensive teams were the most successful teams of their times. In this regard, the point is very clear: defense breeds successful teams.

CHAPTER SUMMARY

As has often been proposed in this book, defense has had more creative thinking, more theories of play, and more adjustments to the new rules that have frequently shaped the play of the game than has offense.

The game of basketball was invented by Dr. Naismith before the turn of the 20th century. Its technical advancements were few until the mid-'20s. Basketball was intended as a recreation sport to be played inside when inclement weather ruled out outdoor games. Coaches at the college level were often assistant football coaches with minimal interest in basketball or the advancement of the game. One Big Ten school had 18 basketball head coaches in 21 years. Obviously, it was not a very important sport on the athletic department's agenda of that institution.

In the late '20s, the NABC was first formed, led principally by Phog Allen, a great coach and a leader in promoting basketball nationally. Joining him was a famous former player and seasoned coach, Nat Holman. Phog was the University of Kansas coach, and Holman, considered the top coach in the East, coached CCNY.

The game was badly in need of sound decision making. In the East, rules interpretations very often differed from the rules interpretations in the Midwest, South, and Far West. Because cross-country travel was very limited, this situation was not a real problem at the time. After World War II, however, travel methods changed dramatically. Teams could now travel to New York from Los Angeles more quickly than they used to get from Los Angeles to San Francisco. The variances of rules interpretations from one part of the country to another caused real problems for traveling teams. The NABC was the leader in standardizing the interpretations that previously created problems for teams visiting other areas.

One instance alone could give real credence to the origination of the NABC. Basketball coaches, rather than coaches of other sports, became the head coaches of athletic departments. The eminence of coaches Phog Allen and Nat Holman began to catch the attention of syndicated sports writers. Some syndicated writers never accepted the game in its earlier stages, and until after the war, they pooh-poohed the game as a spectator sport. The NABC realized that to really promote the game as a spectator sport, creative efforts must be undertaken to guide the game's future. The result was the institution of two very important rules changes. In the mid-'30s, the NABC supported the elimination of the center jump after each basket. They allowed Coach Sam Barry of the University of Southern California and Nibs Pierce of the University of California (Berkeley) to each experiment with a rule that eliminated the jump ball after each made basket. The Pacific Coast Conference (now the Pac 10) was to use this new rule for the entire season. Prior to this rule, the fast-break offense was seldom a force in the outcome of a game. The tempo was seldom upbeat, and the game had little appeal to the average sports spectator. Home arenas, for the most part, were not built or designed to accommodate many spectators other than a few students, alumni, and family.

Because other circumstances—the war, conscription and enlistment—cut down on civilian travel, basketball was at first not able to fully exploit the many virtues of the new rule. In the late '40s, however, the full effect of this rule made itself felt. Its emphasis on speed and athleticism created different thinking when recruiting a basketball player. Equality in size between forwards and guards was shelved as teams began to invert their front and backline players. Guards were the smaller, quicker people charged with running the offense, while the forwards were now rebounding on both boards. Earlier thinking had placed the smaller people both in frontline defense and frontline offense. Soon after the experimentation with the elimination of the center jump rule by the Pac 10, the conference experimented with the 10-second line that is still in place. Prior to the adoption of this center-line rule, some teams preferred not to go upcourt if the defense was playing a zone. Something needed to be done if basketball was to be accepted as a fast-moving, exciting game. As a result, experiments were conducted with the new rule that found it to be an answer to the backcourt slowdown. Little did the NABC know at that time what this rule would mean to the evolution of the game.

Few teams used any type of press defense before the enactment of these two particular rules. One valid reason was that since the inversion concept had never been considered to any extent, the focus of the rule change was to speed up the offensive end of the game. Some of us in the late '40s experimented with the inversion concept. Because our guards, while small, were quick and active, we used the triangle concept on the offensive rebounding and began to bring our defense over the midline and attack these slower-moving offensive guards. The bigger guards were not skilled enough in open-court dribbling to combat the smaller, quicker defenders in the midcourt area. The details of what has been previously explained regarding an offense complementing a defense really brought its advantage into a clear light for me. Because we were positioned to immediately pressure the rebounder and close leads, this tactic gave us a real advantage. Soon, most teams were inverting, and the press became a more popular tactic for the coaches. The press has now become an integral part of many defenses.

The inclusion of black players at the college level, a process that began in the '50s, gave even more emphasis to defense. Their athleticism, quickness, and speed created a tempo of play that brought basketball to heights the coaches of my time had never envisioned. The ironic aspect of all of this is that the 10-second line was never considered for its defensive potential. Currently, however, while little creativity exists offensively, considerable defensive creativity evolved from this rule change.

Those coaches who have studied the path and rise of basketball must be cognizant of the unselfish efforts of the early coaches in a game that has become the fastest-growing team sport in the world. The responsibility of all coaches to help guide the game's future and keep it abreast of needed change and reform is tremendously important. To delegate rules proposals and changes in the game to non-basketball people who thrive on being committee members can misdirect the game.

A vivid example of such misdirection can be seen when the constant drop in the excitement of the NBA game is analyzed. To a great extent, the input of NBA coaches is not appreciated or encouraged. Self-serving people want rules changes that better assist their teams but not the game as a whole. The result: a static, stagnant game that has had no rules change since the adoption of the 24-second rule. (The three-point concept was an ABA rule initially.)

Without question, the game of basketball is great. However, it's great because coaches made it great. They unselfishly gave time and substantial personal effort to keep the game thriving and in balance. Those who truly love the game should not allow self-serving coaches, or people in the media, to force change to accommodate themselves. Coaches should be mindful of suggestions that could better the game, and fully weigh the worth of these suggestions. All coaches should realize that their opinion and input do matter, whether they're a coach of a junior high girls' or boys' team or a coach of a high-profile Division I men's or women's program. Above all, coaches should be creative. Every coach has a voice that should be used to help take the game to even greater heights.

CHAPTER 11

CONCLUSION

The impact that defense has on the outcome of a game or a season must never be under-estimated by a coach. It's true, a team must score points to win a basketball game, but if its defense allows opponents easier shots and more of them, the chances of success are minimal. Of course, instances occur when the offense helps the defense. Complementing the defense with a balanced rebound recovery and court balance has been described as to its importance, but the defense assists the offense in more numerous ways. Loose-ball recoveries, interceptions, quick conversions from defense to offense because of proper vision and enhanced mental alertness are benefits the defense affords the offense.

Tempo is an important facet of basketball. A rule a coach should constantly strive to follow is to play the game at a tempo at which the coach's team can play better than the opponent. As much as some coaches try to convince themselves that they can force a desirable tempo through offensive effort, it is a premise that too often falls short. If a desirable tempo is as important as many coaches feel it is, then the relative importance of defense should be given the attention it deserves.

A team can have the physical talent and depth to be an outstanding fast-tempo team. It would need speed, athleticism and the ability to finish a fast break or to spot up and effectively shoot from the three-point range. The chances of the talented team to de-fend a less-talented team are greatly reduced if the superior team plays a soft, fallback type of defense. The lesser-talented team is better suited to play at a slower tempo and execute well in their half-court game. No matter how much the better-talented team wants an up-tempo game, the opponent will usually control the ball and the tempo. This example is often what is seen when heavily favored teams are unexpectedly upset. Tempo is usually the dominant cause.

Basketball is, in a sense, a contradictory game. Coaches try to teach players offen-sive foot skills, proper mechanics of ball protection, how to create space for their shots, and other individual aspects of offensive play. We have only one ball and five players on a team. We try to develop individualism and at the same time stress the importance of team play. Scoring on offense is the "I" and "me" of basketball. Defense is the "we and us" of the game. Bridging these differing attitudes is not an easy task. Some teams and coaches seem to do it, while other fall short. What is the "why" of it?

It is my belief that a strong, aggressive and successful defensive team manages to get a spillover of its "we and us" concept. As a result, the "I" and "me" offensive thinking becomes much less of a problem. If a defender dives on the floor for the recovery of a loose ball and passes to a teammate, the chance of a selfish play, a faulty-shot selection or a careless pass is greatly reduced. If a teammate takes a hard charge or has caused a foul charged on the opponent, better ball care will usually ensue. When teammates assist each other on defense with good communication and help, better offensive screens seem to follow because of this defensive attitude. Subsequently, the feeling of team play and the practice of defensive help often permeate the team when it converts to offense.

It is more than a coincidence that, at all levels of team play, the top teams are those that are fundamentally sound defensively and take a real pride in their defense. The media will evaluate offense, in most instances, by their point scoring. In basketball, it's the points the star players scored that make the box scores, while defenders are seldom given individual credit for their efforts. A successful defensive effort is attributed not to individuals but to an entire team. This factor gives further proof to the "we" and "us" theory. Teams tend to take real pride in their team accomplishments. Often, playing well defensively is the start of a basketball team acquiring team pride. As a coach, I feel that a team should feed on mutual defensive accomplishments, which will result in unselfishness and pride in their total team play.

photo courtesy Steve Hathaway

Pete Newell is widely considered and respected as one of the greatest coaches in the history of the game. His contributions to basketball span almost six decades. Among his numerous accomplishments are the fact that he is the first basketball coach to have ever won a National Invitation Tournament Championship (University of San Francisco, 1949), an NCAA Championship (University of California—Berkeley, 1959), and an Olympic gold-medal (the United States team in Rome, 1960).

Born in Vancouver, British Columbia, Pete grew up in the Los Angeles area. He graduated in 1939 from Loyola Marymount where he played on both the basketball and baseball teams. Prior to enlisting in the Navy in 1942, he began his coaching career at St. John's Military Academy in Los Angeles. Following his naval service in 1946, he began his college coaching career at the University of San Francisco. After four very successful years as the head coach of the Don's men's basketball program, he then spent four seasons in the same position at Michigan State University.

In 1954, he took over the men's basketball program at the University of California-Berkeley—a position he held until 1960. While he was the Bear's coach, his teams were conference champions for four consecutive years and went to the NCAA Final Eight for four years in a row.

From 1960-68, Pete served as the Director of Athletics at the University of California-Berkeley. He then accepted the position of general manager for the San Diego Rockets (subsequently the Houston Rockets)—a job he held from 1968-71. He worked in the same capacity for the Los Angeles Lakers from 1972-74. Subsequently, he has served as a consultant for both the Golden State Warriors and the Cleveland Cavaliers.

Pete has continued to be actively involved with basketball over the years. Since 1961, he has worked with the Japanese basketball program at both the junior national and the national level and has traveled to Japan in that capacity at least once annually for the past forty years. In 1998, he received the Order of the Sacred Treasure from Emperor Hiro Hito. He has also conducted numerous coaching clinics worldwide, including clinics held both in Europe and in South America. He has served on both the U.S. Olympic Basketball

Committee and the NCAA Tournament Committee. In 1992-'93, he directed an Olympic developmental camp for women post players in Colorado Springs. He continues to act as an adviser to basketball coaches at all competitive levels. He annually conducts his world-renowned "Big Man" camps to teach the fundamentals of post play to both aspiring and proven players.

Pete currently resides in Santa Fe, California. He has four sons, Pete Jr., Tom, Roger, and Greg.